Man of Vision

Man of Vision

Arkansas Education and the Legacy of Arch Ford

BUTLER
CENTER
BOOKS

The Butler Center for Arkansas Studies
Central Arkansas Library System
100 Rock Street
Little Rock, Arkansas 72201

www.butlercenter.org

First edition: August 2016
ISBN 978-1-935106-19-7

Manager: Rod Lorenzen
Book & cover design: Mike Keckhaver
Copyeditor: Ali Welky

Cataloging-in-Publication data is available through the Library of Congress.

Butler Center Books, the publishing division of the Butler Center for Arkansas Studies, was made possible by the generosity of Dora Johnson Ragsdale and John G. Ragsdale Jr.

Printed in the United States of America

This book is printed on archival-quality paper that meets requirements of the American National Standard for Information Sciences, Permanence of Paper, Printed Library Materials, ANSI Z39.48-1984.

Table of Contents

Acknowledgements

Everyone has been extremely kind in helping me write this book and get it ready for publication. I would like to thank the wonderful people at the University of Arkansas Libraries Special Collections who assisted me as I looked through the scrapbooks in the Arch Ford Collection. I would also like to thank Aryn Denette at the University of Central Arkansas Archives for her invaluable help in finding resources about Arch Ford. Special thanks also go to Sue Owens, executive director of Economics Arkansas, and Kathy Moore, administrative manager of Economics Arkansas, who allowed me to spend a day with them going through the Arkansas Council on Economic Education files. They also permitted me to use many of the organization's pictures. Thanks to Mary Clark, chief information officer at UACCM, and Trevor Mize, graphic/web designer at UACCM, for their assistance in getting pictures of the Petit Jean Vo-Tech dedication. I would especially like to thank Joe and Scott Ford, who took the time to read the manuscript and give me feedback. They were both very supportive and encouraging. Finally, I would like to thank the Butler Center for Arkansas Studies and Butler Center manager David Stricklin for agreeing to publish this book. Butler Center Books' manager Rod Lorenzen helped get the manuscript ready, Ali Welky did the copyediting and proofreading, and Mike Keckhaver did the layout and design.

Preface

When I recently retired from my thirty-year adventure of teaching history and economics to high school students, I began to ponder what the next chapter in my life would be. I also started to reflect on my teaching years and the changes that had taken place in education in Arkansas since I began teaching.

Last spring, my brother, Robert Burnett, asked me to create a narrative from his research on the East Fork Masonic Lodge, located in nearby Wooster, Arkansas. It was while I was working on this project that I became curious about one of the lodge's longtime members, Arch Ford.

After my years in Arkansas education, his name was familiar. Not only is the Department of Education building at the Arkansas State Capitol in Little Rock named after him, but the regional educational service office at Plumerville is named the Arch Ford Education Service Cooperative. Since my school district is part of its service area, I had been there on numerous occasions for workshops.

So I started doing some research. I quickly found out that Arch Ford had been born and raised in Wooster. There is also a street in Wooster named after his family. I also found out that he attended Conway High School, which was my alma mater and where had I taught for the past thirty years. He then attended Arkansas State Teachers College (ASTC—now the University of Central Arkansas), from which I received my BSE and MA degrees in history. He, too, majored in history and became a teacher.

After teaching at a handful of schools around Arkansas, Arch Ford became an educational advisor at a Civilian Conservation Corps (CCC) camp before going to work at the Arkansas Department of Education. During his tenure at the Department of Education, Ford collected newspaper clippings and other memorabilia and placed them into scrapbooks. He later donated them to the University of Arkansas Special Collections. After looking through his seventy-five scrapbooks, I began to realize what an impact Ford had on Arkansas education. I also began to realize how much his work had affected my life and the lives of countless others.

My husband, Ron, teaches at the University of Arkansas Community College at Morrilton, which was formerly Petit Jean Vo-Tech, the second of twenty-three vocational-technical centers to open during Ford's tenure. Vocational education also expanded in high schools, including the Conway Area Career Center on my high school campus.

In the early 1960s, Arch Ford and Bessie Moore established the Arkansas Council on Economic Education, which was soon recognized as one of the top economic programs in the nation. It provided training in economics education to thousands of Arkansas teachers and Arkansas's teachers would sweep national awards for teaching economics. As the economics teacher at Conway High School for thirty years, I benefited greatly from the resources and support of this organization.

The Arkansas Children's Colony's opening in 1959 provided its new director, David Ray, with a platform to advocate for public education for special-needs children. Arkansas would train teachers and expand special education programs through the rest of Arch Ford's tenure and beyond. My nephew is one of a growing number of autistic children who receive services that would not have been available a generation ago.

In the 1960s, the Arkansas Educational Television Network (AETN) began airing instructional programming. Arkansas also began funding public kindergarten. Free textbooks would be provided for high school students after years of campaigning by Arch Ford and the Department of Education. All of these advances helped improve education in Arkansas.

The biggest challenge Commissioner Ford faced, however, was obtaining funding for education. When he first joined the state Department of Education, there were about 1,900 school districts and 43% of the state's 406,199 students did not have access to a quality high school education. Approximately 100,000 students had no high school at all in their district. Average teacher pay for the 1947–48 schoolyear was $1,548, and many of those teachers had little or no college training. The Department of Education's annual budget had risen to $425 million by the 1978–79 school year, the year Ford retired. This was over half of the entire state budget. There were only 382 school districts in 1978, and average teachers' salaries were around $14,970 a year. All of Arkansas's certified teachers had at least a bachelor's degree and many had a master's degree. A few even had doctorates.

Arkansas's educational system has often been criticized when compared to that of other states. But Arch Ford built an educational system from the ground up in a state that had one of the lowest per capita incomes in the country. Subsequent leaders have built on that foundation. Class sizes have been reduced, teachers' salaries have increased, and teacher quality has continued to improve. The average teacher salary for Arkansas in 2014 was $48,017, while the 2014 average per capita income for Arkansas was $36,423.[1]

Arch Ford cared very much for the children of Arkansas. He saw education as the door to a better future. As a student in Arkansas schools, I (and thousands of others) benefited from his vision and his efforts. As a teacher, I hope I was able to pass some of his vision on to my students. I hope you enjoy reading about this man and his accomplishments.

Chapter 1: The Early Years

A nyone who has been in Arkansas education for any length of time has heard the name Arch Ford. The Department of Education Building at the Capitol in Little Rock is named after him, and the regional educational service office at Plumerville is called the Arch Ford Education Service Cooperative. Arch Ford was commissioner for the Arkansas Department of Education from 1953 to 1978, serving five different governors: Francis Cherry, Orval Faubus, Winthrop Rockefeller, Dale Bumpers, and David Pryor. He was not only the longest-serving commissioner in the state of Arkansas, but his tenure exceeded that of any other Department of Education head in the United States. His leadership left Arkansas with a strong educational system that would continue to advance. This was his legacy.

Considering what was going on in education in the mid-twentieth century, one quickly realizes that his job was not an easy one. Just a year after he took the commissioner job, the U.S. Supreme Court handed down the *Brown v. Board of Education* (1954) decision. Then, in 1957, Arkansas garnered nation-wide attention during the desegregation crisis at Little Rock Central High. Interestingly, after the notoriety Arkansas gained from this event, the state actually went on to integrate its schools with relatively little resistance. Arch Ford and the Department of Education led the state in making sure there were "no more Little Rock Centrals."

Much attention was given to integration and creating unitary school districts during this time, but, outside of the spotlight, great advances were being made in Arkansas education. Arkansas opened the first of twenty-three vocational-technical schools, Arkansas Vocational-Technical School (now SEARK) at Pine Bluff in 1959. The second, Petit Jean Vocational-Technical School (now UACCM), was opened in 1963. Eventually there would be vocational-technical training within driving distance to anyone in the state. Vocational education was also expanded at the high school level to include more technical training.

In the early 1960s, Arkansas developed one of the best economic education programs in the country. The Arkansas Council on Economic Education (now Economics Arkansas) was formed in 1962 and was soon recognized as one of the top programs in the nation. The organization would provide training in economic education to thousands of elementary and secondary teachers in the state. Arkansas's teachers swept national awards for teaching excellence in the area of economics, and other states modeled their programs after the one in Arkansas.

The Arkansas Children's Colony (now the Conway Human Development Center) opened at Conway in 1959, giving children with mental disabilities a better place to go than the State Hospital or the state's four reform schools. Its new director, David Ray, would then use his position as a platform to advocate for public education for the large percentage of mentally handicapped children who did not need to be institutionalized but instead needed to be educated. Under Commissioner Ford's guidance, Arkansas would train teachers and expand special education programs through the rest of his tenure and beyond.

Arkansas Educational Television Network (AETN) went on the air in 1966 following twelve years of planning. It provided Arkansas children with instructional television as well as popular children's shows such as "Sesame Street" and "Mister Rogers' Neighborhood." Public kindergarten was made possible through a 1968 amendment to the Arkansas Constitution that allowed five-year-olds to be educated by the state. Free textbooks would finally be provided to high school students in 1967 after years of campaigning on the part of Arch Ford and the Department of Education. All of this due to the leadership of Commissioner Ford.

The biggest challenge Commissioner Ford faced, however, was improving the quality of Arkansas education. When he first joined the state Department of Education, Arkansas had about 1,900 school districts, and 43% of the state's 406,199 students did not have access to a quality high school education. Approximately 100,000 students had no high school at all in their district. Average teacher pay for the 1947–48 school year was $1,548, and many of those teachers had little or no college training. Commissioner Ford and the Department of Education raised the educational requirements for Arkansas teachers so that all teachers had at least a bachelor's degree from an accredited college. Throughout his career, he would campaign tirelessly to increase teacher salaries and education funding so that Arkansas could offer a quality education to all.

The Tom Ford Family

The man who would lead Arkansas education during its formative years was raised in Wooster, a small rural town in Faulkner County, Arkansas. It is located about ten miles north of Conway. Most of the people in the area during Ford's childhood farmed cotton and corn. Arch Ford's parents were both raised on farms nearby. Their families had come to the area in the 1880s. George Washington Ford, Arch's grandfather, was the pastor at the nearby Bethlehem Baptist Church. Thomas Francis Clements, his maternal grandfather, had a farm just west of Wooster.

Arch Ford's parents, Thomas Noah Ford (1872–1959) and Minnie Lee Clements (1880–1954), were married in 1898. The couple lived on an eighty-eight-acre hill farm two miles north of Wooster. In addition to being a farmer, Tom Ford was also a Baptist minister. Archibald Washington Ford, called Arch, was born on January 25, 1906. He was the fourth child and second son. He was named after

Thomas Noah Ford and Minnie Lee Clements Ford. *Photo courtesy of Joe T. Ford*

his grandfather, George Washington Ford.

Maud A. Ford (1896–1973) was Arch Ford's oldest sister. At some point she changed her name to Albina and was called Bina by friends and family. She married Oscar L. Moore (1893–1930) on September 27, 1919, in Mayflower, Arkansas. He was a World War I veteran. She became a registered nurse. They had three children: Valta, Leland, and Joe.

Arch's brother Tollie Forrest Ford (1899–1966) served in World War I. He married Oda Jane Williams in 1919, and both attended Arkansas State Teachers College (now the University of Central Arkansas—UCA) in the mid-1920s. He had two step-children, Waymon and John Harris, and one son, Bobby Ford. He was elected tax assessor for Faulkner County in 1931 and served two terms. In 1949, he was elected Faulkner County circuit clerk and served for four terms. He was a candidate for Faulkner County judge in 1956 and 1960. He operated a dairy and beef cattle farm in Wooster after he left office. He also was in real estate and owned Wood Manufacturing Company, a fishing-lure company in Conway.

Ola Lee Ford (1902–2002) was a housewife and also worked ten years at the Arkansas School for the Blind. She married John Henry Glover (1899–1964) in Conway on August 10, 1919. They had nine children: Halogene, Gedria, Gwineva, Robbie, Max, Betty, John, Norma, and James. Her father-in-law, Gus Glover, had one of the first cars in Wooster and owned the first service station in town. The Glover family owned a store, a gristmill, and a blacksmith shop in

Ford house in Wooster, ca. 1917. *Left to right*: Albina Ford Moore, Thomas Noah Ford, Ola Ford Glover, Minnie Clements Ford, Floy Ford Patton Berry, Arch Ford, and Tollie Ford. *Photo courtesy of Joe T. Ford*

Wooster. John and Ola Glover were charter members of First Baptist Church Wooster, which was organized in 1916. When Ola died at age 100, she had been a member for eighty-seven years. The church steeple light was installed and lit in her honor on her 100th birthday.

After Arch was born, there were two more daughters born to Tom and Minnie Ford: Floy Ford Patton Berry (1908–1992) and Avanell Ford Browning Hankins (1919–2011). Floy taught at several different schools, including Greenbrier. She had two daughters, Jean and Mary. Avanell married Elbert Hankins after her first husband, Roy Leo Browning, died after a fall from a horse. She had one son, Tommy Browning.

It was tough making a living on the hill farm, but Tom Ford was determined to obtain an education for his children. He sent three of his children, Ola, Arch, and Floy, to college. "My father was a strong believer in education. He spent pretty well everything he made to keep us in school," Arch said in a 1979 interview. "Father said often, 'I would live on bread and water to keep the kids in school if I had to.'"[2]

In addition to being a Baptist minister and serving in his church as a deacon for over fifty years, Tom Ford's other chief interest was the development of better schools in Faulkner County. He served on the local school board as well as the Faulkner County Board of Education. One of Tom Ford's greatest accomplishments as a member of the local school board was helping raise the school tax from seven mills to twelve mills. After Amendment 40 was passed in 1948 to lift the ceiling on property taxes, he helped raise the tax to 18 mills. But all of that was accomplished after his son Arch had already finished his formal education.

As a member of the Faulkner County Board of Education in the 1930s, Tom Ford helped lead the effort to consolidate the 100 school districts in the county into seven districts. By 1930, twenty small schools in northern Faulkner County, including Wooster, had been consolidated with the Greenbrier district. This allowed for the establishment of the first rural high school in the county. Until that time, Conway was the only district to have a high school. After consolidation, the Greenbrier district would have 1,065 students and was considered the largest district in Arkansas both in area and number of students. But by that time, Arch had already graduated from college. This consolidation also took place before the state School Reorganization Act of 1948 required the consolidation of districts with fewer than 350 students.[3]

Tom Ford was considered progressive in other matters as well. As a community leader, he took a stand on other local issues such as the stock law, the dipping vats (a federal tick-eradication program for the prevention of Texas tick fever in cattle), and the old road improvement districts that were subsequently taken over by the Martineau Road Law. All these progressive movements met with widespread disfavor at the onset, but he had the courage to stand up for them.[4]

Early Education

Arch's education began in the fall of 1912 at the two-room

"academy" at Wooster. As a six-year-old, he walked almost a mile every day to attend. His first teacher was Miss Alice Wilkerson of Beryl.[5] Called the Burks School, the academy was founded around 1888 about one mile east of Wooster. Andrew J. Burks donated the land, which stood in a bend in the road. Traffic could be seen from three directions, which could be a major distraction for students. At one time, someone painted the lower panes of the windows so the children could not look out. It made a lot of people angry and the panes were soon broken out.

According to A. E. Pearson, who attended the Burks School from 1890 to 1904, graded schools had not been heard of at that time. There were no report cards and no exams. Children were promoted when that grade's reader wore out and the student had to buy a new one. Textbooks were not provided by the state.[6]

Lunch for the young Arch Ford was often a big baked sweet potato, hog sausage, and biscuits left over from breakfast. These items were carried in a five-pound lard bucket. Lunch was washed down with a cold drink of water from the well.

The original schoolhouse was blown away by a tornado April 30, 1911. The tornado passed through Plumerville and Wooster that night. Luther Holloway, a strong advocate of education in Wooster and a member of the school board, led the drive to rebuild. Another school was also built in the area around the same time. Residents referred to them as the "little school" and the "big school." Arch's sister, Ola, recalled in a 1999 interview that her brother Arch "felt so proud when he got promoted from the little school to the big school."[7]

The school term was usually only about five or six months. Students would go in the winter months and maybe a month in the summer after the crops were planted. Often the reason for the short terms was the lack of funds. It was very difficult to raise money to run the schools. Pearson said that when he attended Burks School, there was so much opposition to a tax for free schools that the school board would not even buy heater wood for the old potbellied stove. The children gathered chunks of wood and limbs that could be broken by hand. There were not even outhouses; the boys used the woods to the northwest and the girls used the woods to the northeast.[8]

In January 1919, Tom Ford moved his family to Konawa, Oklahoma, a town that had about 1,200 people. Tom joined his brother Joseph Perley Ford and a man named Charley Collins in owning and operating a mercantile store, the largest in Konawa. During summer vacation and on Saturdays, Arch, then thirteen, drove a one-horse delivery wagon twice a day. In his spare time, he played baseball and checkers. He said in a 1954 interview that he thought he might still play a fair game if he had time.[9]

While in Konawa, Arch was able to attend a nine-month school for the first time. He started seventh grade there and graduated as valedictorian of his eighth-grade class before the family moved back to Wooster. In the 1920s, an eighth-grade education was considered the norm. High school at that time was just considered "icing on the cake" by most people, Ford said in a 1977 interview.[10]

In 1920, after the election of Warren G. Harding as U.S. president, the price of cotton fell from 45 cents to 6 cents. The store lost thousands of dollars, and Tom Ford almost went broke. In August 1921, he sold his interest in the store and headed back to Wooster. He bought a farm near the place where the family had lived before.

High School

After the family returned to Wooster, Arch Ford wanted that "icing on the cake." The only high school in Faulkner County in 1921 was in Conway, so Arch saddled up every morning and rode his black pony eight miles across the Cadron Creek to Conway. He left his pony in the wagon yard, paying 5 cents a day to board it while he attended classes at Conway High School. He was not tardy to school even once.

If the weather was too bad, usually for about two months out of the year, he would board in town with Mr. and Mrs. George McClain for $10 a month. Gladys Mobbs of Little Rock, in a 1977 interview, said that her older brothers attended high school with Arch. "As I remember, he had an intensive desire for knowledge and was more or less a bookworm when the other boys were more interested in basketball and baseball."[11]

After a year at Conway High School, Arch attended the training school at Arkansas State Normal School (now UCA) in Conway. He upgraded from a pony to a horse for transportation to Conway. The next year, he and some friends put together money to buy an old Model T Ford so they could drive to school. That was made possible because the newly paved Highway 65 through Conway and Wooster to Martinville was completed about this time. Highway 65 ran down Front Street along the railroad tracks through downtown Conway before it headed through the Cadron Gap and across the bottom land of the East Cadron Creek. A hardwood floor was laid across the King's Bridge, which made it easier to cross the Cadron Creek to make the trip to Conway each day.

Arch finished his high school education at the Normal School. At that time, the teacher training school accepted local students to be taught in a "model school" by college students who were in the training program. If a high school student came to the training school, the administration would determine what classes the student needed to take to make up for deficiencies in his or her high school education. The number of courses the student had to take often depended on the perceived quality of the high school that student had attended before coming to the training school.[12]

Conway was becoming a thriving little town about this time. New buildings were going up everywhere. The Hotel Revilo (later Hotel Bachelor) with sixty-five rooms opened on Front Street in March

1924. The Conway Theatre on Front Street opened up a month later. The Faulkner County Courthouse also underwent a renovation the same year. The Faulkner County Hospital opened in June 1925. Southwestern Bell Telephone Company set up a new 700-line switchboard in 1924; it served 3,000 telephone customers. In 1928, the city also had gas lines installed.

Getting a College Degree

After receiving his high school diploma in 1924, Arch continued his education by taking college courses. It was during this time that the college that would later become UCA changed its name to Arkansas State Teachers College (ASTC). Burr Walter Torreyson was serving at that time as the second president of the institution. He served from 1917 to 1930, presiding over the completion of three major buildings on the campus, including the Administration Building (which would later become Main). A new training school with thirty-three rooms, a gym, a library, and office space was completed in 1925 to replace the Little Green Building.

Arch stayed at ASTC for two years, majoring in education, playing on the basketball team, and working with the debating team. It was during this time that the ASTC basketball program was being developed by Coach Guy "Big Dan" Estes. In the 1925 ASTC *Scroll*, the basketball coach, Coach E. L. Wray, said, "If one should ask me what constituted a good basketball team, I would show him the [ASTC] regulars....Then I would show him McCutcheon, Mabrey, Charles, Smith and Ford, all of them ready for the forward position at any time. It would be next to impossible to point out to him the best pair for the job."[13] While attending ASTC, Arch stayed at a boarding house built by a fellow student, Ben T. Laney, who had struck oil in Ouachita County. The enterprising Laney would later become governor of Arkansas.

Furthering his education was expensive, and Arch sometimes ran short of funds. He occasionally borrowed money from Mr. Jim Patton, who ran a store in Wooster. He would borrow against the future cotton crop, and the debt was always paid off each fall. Financially he was always running a year behind. To catch up, he dropped out of college for one year and taught at Turrell High School in Crittenden County.

At Turrell, he taught history and mathematics. The first class he taught was algebra. He wasn't sure he knew any algebra, and he was definitely sure he didn't know how to teach. "I was scared to death," he said in a 1954 interview.[14] In addition to teaching, he also served as the athletic director, the coach, and a school bus driver. His salary was $125 a month. He did well enough to be renewed for the next year but chose to go back to college to finish his degree.

The other, more compelling, reason he decided to return to college was that he had fallen in love. He had met Ruby Lee Watson (1908-2005) at a country picnic two years earlier. He saw her drinking a red soda pop and he was hooked. "I was in love," he said. "I wanted to be where I could see Ruby Lee." They married on Christmas Eve 1927.[15] Between them, they had five dollars to spend on the wedding. After paying the preacher three dollars, they each had a dollar to spend. Neither later remembered what they spent it on. "I know one thing," Arch said. "We didn't keep them."[16] Mr. Watson gave his daughter a cow for a wedding present so the new couple would be off to a good start (or at least have milk).

The Watson Family

Ruby Watson Ford's family descended from Irish ancestry that has been traced back to 1641. Her grandfather, Samuel Thomas Watson (1837-1910), had a newspaper in the early days of Old Lewisburg, an early thriving town near Morrilton. It was well known that he disliked both the English and the Yankees. As long as he lived, he would not wear a blue shirt or suit because blue reminded him of

Arch Ford in his
basketball uniform. He
was captain of the team
in 1926. *Photo courtesy of
Arch Ford Collection, UA
Special Collections*

the "Damyankees" who captured him at Gettysburg.[17]

Ruby's father, Samuel Webster Watson (1883-1947), was postmaster of Greenbrier from 1934 to 1935 and served as the Union Township committeeman for a number of years. He also served as chair of the Faulkner County Central Committee. He married Ermon Kirkpatrick (1885-1975) on November 8, 1903, and they had ten children, of which nine survived. Ruby's brother Raymond Faber (1908-1986), served as county clerk of Faulkner County. Her other brothers were Ules Samuel (1918-2002), Joe Deal (1922-1992), and Sam T. Watson, Jr. (1915-1977). Her sisters were Floy Hargrove (1904-1995), Wilma Vann (1911-2003), Jimmie Lee Smith Gean (1924-2005), and Meredith Lowenstein (1917-1993).

With the help of his parents, Arch was able to continue his education. The ASTC *Scroll* in 1928 lists him as a member of Sphinx, captain of the basketball team in 1926, a member of the debating team in 1926 and 1928, and in the YMCA and Historical Society, saying, "Archie is a conscientious and successful student, and is liked by everyone. His presence will be missed on the [ASTC] Campus."[18] Arch spoke of his debating experience in a 1954 interview, saying, "I regard my training as a debater under Dr. D. D. McBrien as the most valuable part of my college career."[19] In his junior and senior years, Arch Ford entered the inter-collegiate debate. He lost the first year and won the second.

He marched with the ASTC graduating class of 1928 but did not

1925 Arkansas State Teachers College basketball team. *Top row*: Coach Wray, Ferguson, McCutcheon, Clark, Holeman, Thomas, Purifoy, Fair, Coach Estes
Middle Row: Cox, Charles, Ford, Adams (captain), Mabrey, Smith, Henderson
Bottom Row: Dejarnett, Shumate, Beard, Kessenger, L. Patton, D. Patton, Griffin.
Photo courtesy of UCA Archives

get his diploma until years later because he was short two hours of credits. College officials let him walk with the promise that he would finish the two hours by correspondence, but it was several years before he finally finished the work. After completing his degree in education at Arkansas State Teachers College, Arch Ford would go on to get his MA in vocational education and a Diploma for Advanced Study in educational administration (1965) from the University of Arkansas (UA) in Fayetteville. He graduated with the highest possible grade, an A or 6.0, in his master's program, which means that each of the examiners rated him at the top in every subject. He also was awarded an honorary PhD from Ouachita Baptist University in 1962.

When Arch Ford was chosen to head the State Education Department, Dr. Henry Kronenberg, dean of the UA College of Education, said, "Mr. Ford is one of our outstanding graduates. He knows the problems and program of education in Arkansas, and has a sufficient amount of practical ingenuity to direct the many forces interested in and concerned with public schools....I believe that Mr.

Ford is one of the best suited people in the state for the job."[20]

Early Teaching Positions

It was not originally Arch's plan to be a teacher. He wanted to study law. But after college, he took a job teaching vocational agriculture in Holland. The community had just built a new six-room schoolhouse. It stood on the site of the present-day city park. There were 300 children attending school in Holland at that time. Holland consolidated with Greenbrier in the 1950s.

Arch then taught in Morgantown in Van Buren County. Teachers in Arkansas were once paid in warrants that were taken to the local banks. The banks would then have to redeem them at the courthouse. Former Van Buren County sheriff J. W. Hatchett, father of former State Police director Lindsey Hatchett, kept Arch going by cashing his warrants and hoping there would be money later to redeem them.

While Arch was teaching in Morgantown, the county superintendent, R. L. Taylor, was invited to deliver the graduation address. A cloudburst fell just before the ceremony, and the motor of Taylor's car was drowned out in a creek. He never arrived, so Arch was recruited to give the address. Arch said, "It didn't make any difference about the speech, the youngsters and their parents were there for those diplomas."[21] In an *Arkansas Democrat* editorial in 1953, the editor relayed a story Arch had told him about how often teachers would be called upon to perform a funeral for a small child because there were no ministers or other officials present.[22] That was an especially tough task, but it had to be done.

Arch next took a teaching position at Mountain Pine. The following term, he taught at Lakeside High School in Garland County, where some hard cash (rather than warrants) was available. He then quit teaching to begin working for the Civilian Conservation Corps.

Chapter 2: Civilian Conservation Corps

I n 1935, Arch Ford became an educational advisor for the Civilian Conservation Corps (CCC), working out of the CCC camp in Jacksonville, Arkansas. The camp at Jacksonville was one of the largest and finest of these camps that operated during the Depression. It was established on April 4, 1933.[23]

The CCC camps were created during the Depression to give work to young men, ages eighteen to twenty-five, and to undertake conservation efforts in America's parks, forests, and farmlands. By the time the program was phased out at the beginning of World War II, more than three million men had served terms of six months or more.

Civilian Conservation Corps in Arkansas

Arkansas had an average of thirty-seven camps in operation between 1933 and 1942. At the height of the program, there were sixty-four camps. A total of 69,038 Arkansans were enrolled in the CCC, and another 6,511 served as technical personnel. The average enrollee was nineteen years old, had eight years of education, and was part of a family that was on the relief rolls. A young man earned $30 per month, with $25 of that mandated to be sent home to his family.[24]

During the time these young men worked in Arkansas CCC camps, 4,956 bridges were built, 5,288 miles of truck trails and back roads were forged, and 82,190 check dams and other erosion-control measures were put in place. These men planted 19,463,745 trees and made major strides in fire prevention in Arkansas's forests. Some of the state parks built by the CCC men were Petit Jean, Mount Nebo, Crowley's Ridge, Devil's Den, Lake Catherine, White Rock Mountain, and Buffalo Point. Boyle Park and Fair Park in Little Rock were also constructed by the CCC men. All told, the CCC spent

$65 million in mostly capital improvements throughout the state of Arkansas.

Besides these visible legacies of the CCC camps, there are some less tangible ones. Once the camps were up and running, some CCC administrators began to realize that the concentration of large numbers of poor and usually unskilled young men provided a wonderful opportunity to provide education and job training so that the men would be more employable when they left the camps. Some administrators began to talk about the possibility of a more advanced educational program, including university extension courses. Eventually, in the fall of 1933, a recommendation was made to name a CCC director who would be in charge of all educational activities in the camps.[25]

Arch Ford in his Civilian Conservation Corps uniform. He was an educational advisor at the CCC camp in Jacksonville, Arkansas. *Photo courtesy of Arch Ford Collection, UA Special Collections*

Education in CCC Camps

What emerged was a program in which the Office of Education in the Interior Department appointed a director of CCC education. This director would appoint advisers for each of the camps. The camp educational adviser would choose one enrollee to serve as his assistant, receiving an extra $6 a month in pay.

The objectives of the CCC education program were to 1) eliminate illiteracy 2) raise the level of enrollees deficient in school subjects 3) provide instruction on camp work jobs and projects 4) provide vocational training 5) provide training in constructive and worthwhile use of leisure time 6) provide cultural and general education 7) provide training in health, first aid, and safety 8) provide character and citizenship training, and 9) assist enrollees in finding employment.[26]

A survey of the educational level of enrollees revealed that there were more than 10,000 illiterate men nationwide in the camps. Over 50% of the enrollees had never finished eighth grade. While 46% of enrollees nationwide had attended some high school, only one third of those had graduated. Slightly more than 3% of the enrollees had gone to college, but only one-fifth of 1% had actually graduated from college.

The duties of the camp educational adviser were to: 1) provide general supervision of educational activities in the camp 2) develop an educational program suited to the needs and interests of men in the camp 3) secure supplemental education facilities from schools, colleges, and other organizations in the area 4) supervise the work of the assistant leaders for education 5) recommend to the company commander opportunities for coordinating the education program with the work and recreational programs, and 6) advise and counsel the enrollees on their educational program and vocational development.

In many camps, the camp commander and educational adviser would organize a Committee on Education, composed of camp military, technical, and educational personnel. This committee would meet weekly to discuss educational problems and find ways to solve them. A number of camps would have weekly meetings with all the instructors. Instructors were trained in better teaching methods, in lesson planning, and in understanding the enrollees' learning difficulties. CCC area and district advisers would visit the camps at least once a month. There were district conferences every four to six weeks to assist in program development. Many schools and colleges loaned out their training facilities to the CCC, but the training was usually held in the recreation hall, the barracks, or other camp buildings. Camp libraries were set up, with some 417,000 volumes circulating monthly among the camps. Some 10,000 educational films were being shown monthly in the camps. Camp leaders also set up forums and debate groups as well as courses on the duties of citizenship.

When enrollees came into camp for the first time, the educational adviser would interview them to determine their interests and aptitudes. Enrollees with common needs would be grouped together for work under competent leaders. There was some individualized instruction for those who needed it. Most courses were organized on a three-month basis. Groups of twelve to fifteen would be given a part to discuss or demonstrate. Study groups were also established.

In addition to offering facilities, local educators also lent their expertise to the CCC camps. School teachers from neighboring towns and local college students would often help with instruction. School superintendents in neighboring districts helped find materials and facilities. Some colleges granted scholarships or financial aid to enrollees who wanted to go on to college. Colleges also offered correspondence courses. Records indicate that some 5,735 courses were offered to 25,158 enrollees. The Office of Education issued a set of pamphlets to camps giving instruction outlines for different vocations, together with a manual for vocational instructors. Some of the vocational areas were agriculture, auto repair, carpentry, cooking, mechanical drawing, radio servicing, and plane surveying.

By 1936, there were 17,523 vocational courses being taught nationwide at CCC camps. Records indicate that 217,039 men were enrolled in these courses. Many camps also organized clubs for studying gardening, poultry, livestock management, and dairying. Records were kept in enrollees' cumulative records, which were kept confidential and given to the enrollees when they were honorably discharged from the camp. They would then have documentation of the skills, aptitudes, and educational advancements they had made while at the camp. The men would also receive job interview coaching and assistance in letter writing for job applications. There was even a special course on "job getting." The federal government set up a national employment plan to find placements for camp alumni who qualified by virtue of their CCC experience.

Arch and Ruby Ford with sons, Justin (*left*) and Watson (*right*).
Photo courtesy of Joe T. Ford

The CCC in Arkansas was nationally noted for its educational programs. It was reported that more than 2,000 Arkansas enrollees learned to read and write in the CCC. Eighth-grade diplomas, high school credits, and college credits were earned while enrollees were in Arkansas CCC camps. College centers were established near three of the state colleges. More than 5,000 Arkansans completed American Red Cross first-aid courses. In Arkansas, agricultural education programs in the CCC camps were operated through cooperation of the Extension Service and State Vocational teachers. All Arkansas CCC camps had agricultural projects.[27]

In a 1953 interview, Arch Ford said, "I learned more about boys in the CCC than I ever learned any other place, including teaching."[28] Much of his philosophy was formed during the years he worked as an educational advisor for the CCC camps. This experience of interviewing hundreds of boys, he maintains, taught him about poverty and about people in need. "It was during this time that I got interested in counseling and guidance. About three percent of the boys couldn't read or write. My assistant and I taught the best we could. They had to learn to sign the payroll or they wouldn't get their money."[29]

The Depression years were difficult ones for Arch and Ruby Ford. Their two older sons both died during this time. Harold Watson

Ford, born April 10, 1930, died of spinal meningitis at the age of two on October 2, 1932. Justin Turner Ford, born November 2, 1928, was poisoned by wild berries at the age of seven. He passed away on December 9, 1935. Their third son, Joe, was born in 1937 after both of his older brothers had died.

Chapter 3: Arkansas Department of Education

O n May 4, 1941, Arch Ford went to work for the Arkansas Department of Education for $200 a month as a district supervisor of the war training programs in Northwest Arkansas. Ford said, "We went out and built canning kitchens with the home economics people. And we also prepared people to weld and so on in local schools in preparation for what later became the war."[30]

He and his family lived in Conway during this time. The city was still growing and prospering. In 1951, the city's first traffic light was installed, at the intersection of Harkrider and Oak streets. Parking meters were installed downtown to help pay for street repair and new construction. Dean Milk opened in 1952 and Virco Manufacturing, which produced school furniture, opened in 1954. Lake Conway was created south of Conway in 1946 and Lake Beaverfork, created just north of Conway, would become the city's main water supply in 1957.

Formal picture of Arch Ford. *Photo courtesy of www. conwaypedia.net*

The district supervisor job was supposed to be a temporary one, but Ford ended up staying at the Department of Education for over thirty-seven years. In a 1975 interview, he said, "I didn't come here with any intention of staying, really."[31] But stay he did, and his next position was supervisor of vocational education. He worked under the assistant education commissioner. He then became the state supervisor for business education before becoming assistant commissioner himself in 1948. He served in that position under Commissioners Ralph B. Jones (who served 1941–1949) and A. B. Bonds Jr. (1949–1953).

Ford Named Commissioner of Education

The Arkansas Department of Education was created in 1931 with the education commissioner being appointed by the state Board of Education. The board was made up of nine members, appointed by the governor for staggered terms. Ford would be the sixth commissioner[32] to hold the position, and he became the person who held it the longest—twenty-six years.

There had been a complicated political climate during the tenure of Commissioner A. B. Bonds Jr. During the 1952 gubernatorial campaign, in which Judge Francis Cherry defeated incumbent governor Sid McMath in a Democratic primary runoff, Judge Cherry had called for Bonds's dismissal.[33] After Cherry's election, Bonds decided to leave before his term was up. He said, "I just wish there were some way we could get this department out of politics."[34]

The Board of Education, which also wished to take the position "out of politics," offered the job to Arch Ford. Governor-elect Cherry had another person in mind for the post but did not insist on it, and the board unanimously elected Ford.[35] Ford related in a 1978 interview, "The chairman of the Board came to me and said they wanted to professionalize the Department of Education. He said, 'we think you can do that. You've been here long enough and people know you and you have competency in both vocational and general education. The superintendents would like you to take it and the board would like you to take it.'"[36]

In 1954, the education commissioner in Arkansas was responsible for leadership in elementary, secondary, and adult education in the state. The person in this role was the ex-officio secretary and executive officer of the state Board of Education, which was also the state Board of Vocational Education. The commissioner headed the staff of the

Department of Education and assisted the board in implementing and improving educational programs. The commissioner also oversaw the proper accounting of funds and the carrying out of policies of the board.

Ford hesitated before accepting the position. He asked for time and then made the trip to Wooster to seek out his eighty-one-year-old father's advice. "I spent three hours talking about it with him. He advised me about what I could expect if I took the job—remember, this was in 1953—including a Supreme Court decision that would outlaw desegregation. My father said to me, now you can expect the travail that will come to the whole country, particularly the South because it's my opinion that segregation is on its way out in this country. I thought he was a pretty wise man."

The two men also talked about the public, their schools, the board, and the governors. Tom Ford told his son that no man could stay very long unless he could get along with the governor. He said Arch would have to talk to Governor Cherry and tell him that he had supported Governor McMath.[37] "The governor may not directly control that job, but he controls the purse strings, and anybody who controls the purse strings has a lot of power," his father told him.[38]

Ford accepted the job, and his first day as commissioner was January 6, 1953. The salary was $7,500, and there would be many battles to increase it through the years. When he retired in 1978, his salary was $33,020. He would end up working for five different governors, including the first Republican governor since Reconstruction, Winthrop Rockefeller.

"I've never had any problem with governors,"[39] Commissioner Ford maintained. In a 1977 interview, he said, "I've never understood people who can't get along with governors. I've found them easy to get along with. They just want you to do a good job and cooperate with their objectives."[40] He also said in another interview that year,

"I don't worry about my job. I just worry if I'm doing it right." Right, he said, meant providing leadership, leadership for which politicking is undoubtedly the tool and which is exercised "partly through regulations and partly through support."[41]

There were many positive reactions to his appointment. Former commissioner Bonds said, "The choice was made on a strictly professional basis and I foresee a new era of professional status for the Department as a result of this action."[42]

Karr Shannon, known for his editorial columns in the *Arkansas Democrat* at the time, said it was the first time a man thoroughly familiar with the overall public school system was ever named for the top position. "His sole ambition in life has been the profession of teaching; he has no side interests. He knows the score when it comes to the Arkansas school system and has the confidence of teachers and district school board members."[43]

Another editorial in the *Arkansas Democrat* spoke of Commissioner Ford's character. "He is well known, although he shuns publicity that would attract attention to himself. Over the years he has worked with so many school people and other citizens that they can go to the new commissioner with their problems as old friends seeking advice and help. Commissioner Ford will give us plain spoken, practical, unassuming and courageous leadership. Although his primary interest is improving school facilities, he is not prone to single out education and overlook the many other things that likewise need to be advanced in Arkansas."[44]

Dr. T. S. Staples, dean of Hendrix College in Conway from 1928 to 1949, was a member of the Arkansas Board of Education at that time. He probably knew Commissioner Ford better than any of the other board members since he was also from Conway. He said, "A good commissioner must first be a gentleman. Second, he must possess a reasonable amount of industry. Third, he must have courage, and then if he has some book learning, it would help." He added, "By golly, if anything has gone wrong with Arch Ford, it's happened since he left his old Dad."[45]

Dr. Silas Snow, president of Arkansas State Teachers College from 1953 to 1975, said, "I can say as a lifelong friend, college mate, and professional co-worker, Archie Ford, in my opinion, commands universal respect of the professional people and the general lay public throughout Arkansas. Mr. Ford possesses a high degree of integrity, has a keen intellect and his friends are limited only by the number of people with whom he has come in contact. The state Board of Education is to be commended in its election of a career man in the state's Department of Education for commissioner. All of us at Arkansas State Teachers College are proud of this prominent alumnus."[46]

Dr. Henry Kronenberg—dean of the College of Education at the University of Arkansas, where Ford earned his master's degree—said, "Mr. Ford is one of our outstanding graduates. He knows the problems and program of education in Arkansas, and has a sufficient amount of practical ingenuity to direct the many forces interested in and concerned with public schools. The task of keeping our educational forces unified is a tremendous one. And I believe that Mr. Ford is one of the best suited people in the state for this job."[47]

The Department of Education staff was also very pleased with the decision. Dr. Ed McCuistion, who had been with the department since 1931, summed up the feeling of the staff: "It is more important to be respected for what you do and the way you do it than it is to have a lot of learning. The inspiring elements of leadership are those fine, delicate, ingenious qualities of both the mind and the heart.... Those of us who know Arch best have confidence in his sincerity; we are aware of his genuineness....You don't mind talking to Arch Ford about anything and as you do, you become conscious of the nearness of his understanding to yours....He doesn't make a lot of noise, but he does make a lot of headway. Without exception, everyone in the department wishes him well."[48]

Later that year, Commissioner Ford shared a set of objectives that he wanted to accomplish as the new commissioner. They were:

• Develop greater participation by local school administrators and teachers in all phases of the state program. He had appointed an advisory committee of thirty to keep him posted on problems and policies which affect local schools.

• Arrange some reorganization of the department.

• Reduce the amount of non-salary items in the budget.

• Enact a policy of giving all the facts to all the people at all times.

• Develop complete cooperation with General Assembly and Arkansas Legislative Council.

• Assist in creating awareness on the part of the public of the need for increased teachers' salaries.

• Move toward equalization of opportunities to all children in state, including black students.

• Develop more cooperation between state and local governmental units and all groups who deal with children. "The child is one child; he isn't a series of parts."[49]

One of the early things that the department did to increase public awareness was to create a series of Saturday-morning televised programs to try to give the public a greater understanding of the Department of Education. The format was a panel discussion on various facets of department services. The series ran for a few months during the 1959–60 school year.[50]

In 1963, the department also began publishing *Education Newsmagazine*, a monthly publication that kept the public and those in education updated on developments and trends in Arkansas's public schools.[51]

Attempt to Oust Ford

Arch Ford's reputation and his leadership in the Department of Education were the main reasons he was able to continue as commissioner through five governors. There was only one occasion in the twenty-six years he served as education commissioner that anyone ever seriously threatened his job. In December 1960, Representative Paul Van Dalsem of Perry County, chairman of the Arkansas Legislative Council (ALC), tried to use his position to remove Ford from his position as commissioner. Van Dalsem and Ford had exchanged words before in the heat of discussions about educational policy, but some thought this attempt was a result of politics. It was speculated that in the 1960 election, Ford, a resident of Conway, had apparently not sufficiently supported the re-election of Van Dalsem's "Old Guard" colleague, Guy "Mutt" Jones. Jones, state representative from Conway's district, was opposed by one of Commissioner Ford's old friends, Graham T. Nixon. Nixon's family was from the Wooster area, where Ford was raised. Jones was defeated by Nixon not only in 1960 but in 1962 as well. Others said that Ford got caught up in the controversy over an issue with teacher retirement. Governor Faubus suggested that many legislators felt Ford had kept them in the dark regarding the cost of the teacher retirement system.[52]

Van Dalsem, who appeared to have worked behind the scenes, compelled Representative John E. Miller of Izard County to make an amendment to the 1961–1963 education appropriations bill which would require the commissioner of education to have a doctorate degree. Van Dalsem, using his power as chairman, did not encourage any discussion and appeared to be laughing about the situation. He called for a voice vote and then determined that the "ayes" had it. Observers later stated that they could not determine whether the "ayes" had it or not. If there is any question, a show of hands or a roll call vote is usually then taken. But in this case, Van Dalsem, apparently still chuckling, rapped his gavel and announced that the motion had passed. When Ford was asked about the amendment, he replied that he didn't know of any reason Van Dalsem would oppose him. He also noted that some college presidents didn't have a doctorate degree. Other than those two comments, he said he didn't want to talk about it.[53]

Some of Commissioner Ford's supporters on the Legislative Council felt that they had been outmaneuvered and tried to get the issue brought up again. Senator Russell Elrod of Siloam Springs, vice chairman of the ALC, made a motion to reopen the issue, saying he disputed the results of the previous vote. Another senator, Senator Robert Harvey of Swifton, said it was not the job of the Legislative Council to set the standards for Department of Education employees. Senator Elrod had to have sixteen of the twenty-four votes in order to reopen the issue, but he got only thirteen. Ford's job would be up in the air until the legislature met again in January.[54]

A couple of days later, Senator Jones publicly denied any role in the Legislative Council's action against Commissioner Ford. Jones said that neither Ford nor any member of the Legislative Council had said anything to him about what the trouble might be between them. He added that Ford was retained as education commissioner when Governor Orval Faubus took office in 1955 because of an agreement that Jones had made with Faubus. Faubus had agreed to keep Ford if Jones and his friends would support Faubus against incumbent Governor Cherry. Jones also said that he had defended Ford against legislative attacks during the time he was in the legislature.[55]

Newspapers, school superintendents, and school groups came to Commissioner Ford's defense. The state Board of Education took up the matter at its meeting the next week. The board issued a prepared statement praising Commissioner Ford as an "able, dedicated and efficient" administrator and said it had no intention of replacing him. Governor Faubus was shown the prepared statement before its release and said that it "pretty well expressed my views." Ford said after the meeting that he was "gratified" by the board's action. He again declined to discuss the Legislative Council's action.[56]

There was another incident in the Legislative Council a few days later when one of the senators made a motion that Representative Van Dalsem had to produce a certificate proving he had completed the eighth grade before he could take the oath of office for his next term. Van Dalsem shouted, "You're out of order, recess for lunch!" He banged his gavel and walked away red faced and laughing. Van Dalsem was actually one of the best-educated men in the legislature at the time. He had two bachelor's degrees and had completed more than half of the work on a master's degree in agriculture. After he was elected to the legislature to represent Perry County, however, he never returned to complete his master's program.[57]

It would be February 1961 before Ford got any good news about his job. The Joint Budget Committee of the legislature deleted the restriction from the Education Department appropriations bill that would have removed Ford as commissioner. The restriction was removed at the request of Governor Faubus. Representative Van Dalsem gave in to the change but insisted that Ford's salary remain at $10,000. The Board of Education had requested that the salary be increased to $12,000, but Van Dalsem said that the $12,000 figure had been put in the budget based on the commissioner having a doctorate.[58]

The case was not closed on this matter yet. Van Dalsem left the State Capitol early on Thursday afternoon of that week to attend a Legislative Leaders Conference in Ft. Lauderdale, Florida. The Joint Budget Committee met at noon and raised Ford's salary to $10,800.[59] Van Dalsem made no attempt to fight that when he returned, but when the Senate voted to raise Ford's salary to $12,000 the next month, the House refused to agree and stayed with the $10,800 figure.[60]

In an interview after his retirement, Ford said he thought Representative Van Dalsem's move arose from the fact that Representative Mutt Jones was defeated by an old friend of his. Van Dalsem and Jones were allies, and Ford said, "Mutt didn't take his defeat very kindly." In regard to Governor Faubus stepping in to save his job, he said, "There was one thing about the Old Guard. That was that it had a boss—it was the governor." When Faubus said the issue was dead, it was.[61] Not too long after the incident, Ouachita Baptist University awarded Ford an honorary doctorate. He was presented with a doctor of law degree in 1962.[62]

Reorganizing the Department of Education

One of the recurring issues Ford faced as commissioner was the lack of money for public education. On more than one occasion, the governor or the legislature would propose a reorganization of the Department of Education as a way to cut costs and make the department more efficient.

Ford himself had included reorganization of the department as one of his objectives when he became commissioner. The Arkansas Legislative Council, which considers budget requests and makes recommendations to the General Assembly, considered department costs as one of the top three problems facing schools in Arkansas. The council wanted Ford and the Board of Education to take action as soon as possible to reorganize the department.

Just ten months after Ford started his new job, the Arkansas Legislative Council was impatiently demanding that he explain why the Board of Education had not yet acted on a plan to reorganize the department. Representative Van Dalsem of Perry County, who was a member of the Arkansas Legislative Council, said that Ford had assured the council the previous year that "he would personally arrange for a reorganization of the State Department of Education which would reduce personnel, save money and at the same time provide greater services."[63] Van Dalsem introduced a resolution asking that Commissioner Ford explain "what he had in mind and what steps he contemplates." The department had been working on a plan and by the middle of the next month, the Board of Education had acted on Ford's plan to reorganize the Department of Education.

The reorganization reduced the number of people in field services responsible to the commissioner from nine to four; at the same time, it added two that were directly part of the commissioner's office. These two positions were the head of the Statistics and Research Division and the supervisor for Accounting and Disbursements. The primary objectives of the reorganization, Ford said, were to render better services to local schools, make administration more effective, and make the other two posts responsible to the commissioner. The creation of the research division was an answer to the criticism of past years that the Education Department did not have sufficient facts. Centralization of accounting and disbursements was made on the recommendation of the Legislative Audit Committee.

Six people now constituted the heads of the different divisions and all others were directly responsible to those six. Advisory committees were functioning in five of those six divisions. "We don't make any claim to perfection, but we do know we are trying to operate the department economically and effectively," Ford said.[64]

The Department of Education would see growth after the implementation of the National Science Education Act. The Soviet launching of Sputnik, the first man-made satellite, in 1957 prompted Congress to appropriate money to improve science, math, and modern language education in the elementary and secondary schools. In order for the state to qualify for the nearly $1 million in federal aid a year, the Department of Education had to increase its staff to seven.

Five additional supervisors—one a major in science, one a major in math, one a major in modern foreign language, and two with special training in elementary education—were added.[65]

Another reorganization of the department took place in 1966. By this time, the department had grown to twelve divisions, so the board combined them into five new divisions: Finance, Administrative Services, Vocational Services, Instructional Services, and Federal Education Program Services. Each would be headed by an associate commissioner of education, a new title. The new associate commissioners would be chosen by the board on the recommendations of Commissioner Ford. Two divisions, the Rehabilitation Services for the Blind and the Arkansas Rehabilitation Services, were unaffected by the reorganization. The reorganization was implemented in 1967.[66]

The last major reorganization took place during Governor Dale Bumpers's tenure as part of a larger reorganization of state government. The sixty agencies that made up state government were reorganized under thirteen major departments responsible in varying degrees to the governor. Purchasing, budgeting, and related management functions were placed with the heads of the departments. The Board of Education was still given the authority to make policy, but, under the new reorganization, the commissioner (renamed director) nominated by the board would have to meet the approval of the governor. For the rest of Ford's tenure, he had to get written approval to continue as director when a new governor was elected.[67]

In Bumpers's reorganization of state government, the Arkansas Rehabilitation Services and the Rehabilitation Services for the Blind were transferred from the Department of Education and placed under the Department of Social and Rehabilitative Services. The surplus property program was transferred to the Department of Finance and Administration. The Educational Television Commission, the Library Commission, the School for the Blind, and the School for the Deaf were transferred to the Department of Education.[68] One of the benefits of this reorganization was that these agencies had the support of the Department of Education behind them in trying to get the funding they needed.

In *Education Newsmagazine*, November 1978, Ford reflected on the reorganization. "I think it was a must. As far as we are concerned, it has worked extremely well....Reorganization provided an immediate advantage for the small agencies added to Education," he said. "They gained the support of the overall Department for their needs." He pointed to increased budgets and specifically to increased salaries for the employees of the Library Commission. He compared reorganization to school consolidation. "You don't save money, but you make wiser expenditure of money. You make more progress in giving service." He said he thought reorganization helped the legislature as well as the governor by providing more manageable figures to deal with when budgets were presented. However, he said he thought reorganization had just started and needed to be reviewed and improved each biennium. One danger he saw in reorganization was too much concentration of power. He said this could be avoided by retaining the functions of policymaking boards while not making the governor weak.

Arch Ford Education Complex

As the Department of Education changed and grew during the tenure of Arch Ford, often there was not enough space at the Education Building on the State Capitol grounds for all of the offices that were needed. Some of the department offices had to be housed instead in other buildings around Little Rock. In 1969, a major renovation took place to give the department more room. The old State Highway Building west of the Education Building had been vacated when the Highway Department moved into new facilities on Interstate 30. The Department of Education bought it for $400,000 and got a $750,000 appropriation to renovate the building and connect it to the Education Building with a one-story structure. The old Highway Department building had an auditorium which would be quite useful to the Education Department. Two annex buildings at the rear gave the Education Department a five-building complex on the State Capitol grounds.[69] The remodel was completed late that summer, and the Board of Education decided to name the new building complex after Arch Ford at the request of the Senate.[70]

Providing Services to Public School Districts

As Ford neared the end of his tenure as director, the Board of Education authorized a study done by consultants from Southern Arkansas University (SAU). The study determined that the department was not large enough to provide the needed technical assistance to

Arch Ford Education Building. *Photo courtesy of Ron Beckman*

the 385 school districts of Arkansas. While the study drew the usual conclusion that the state needed to consolidate a number of districts to eliminate inefficiencies, there was also a suggestion that a system of regional offices be set up by the department to provide administrative services to school districts.[71]

This came to pass in 1984 when fifteen Education Service Cooperatives were set up. One of them, Arch Ford Education Service Cooperative, services a seven-county area that includes Arch Ford's hometown of Wooster. It is located at Plumerville, where his father was born. Arch Ford spoke to a group of about twenty-five superintendents and other educators at the first official meeting of the cooperative. He said that "education is the pre-eminent profession in the country" and that the profession in the state would eventually reflect recent attempts to improve public education.[72]

Another recommendation of the SAU study was that the governor's power over the director be removed. "This requirement by the law puts the agency head on a potentially political basis, dependent on the thinking of any incoming governor, and places some restraint on his leadership responsibility to public school education in the state. The potential of this restraint has probably not affected the incumbent agency head to the degree that it will affect his replacement because of the incumbent's long years of tenure and service." The consultants suggested that the director should serve at the pleasure of the board "but with assurances of meaningful cooperation with the executive branch of government."[73]

Accolades as a Leader in Education

Throughout his tenure as commissioner of education, Arch Ford received recognition for his leadership in education. In 1958, Ford was named to the 16th Geographical-Vocational Index of *Who's Who in America*. He also joined educational leaders from other states in serving on the Council of Chief State School Officers. In 1958, he was selected to represent the Council of State School Officers on the Committee on Studies of the American Association of Colleges for Teacher Education. He would serve as vice president of the Council of State School Officers before being named president of the council in 1962–63. He later served on its executive board.

He also served as vice chairman of the Southern States Work Conference Committee on Economic Development for the Southern Region. He was chairman of the Arkansas delegation to the White House Conference on Education in 1955 and a member of the Arkansas delegation to the White House Conference on Children and Youth in 1960. He was a charter member of the Executive Committee of the National Education Commission of the States.

In 1964, the Freedoms Foundation at Valley Forge in Pennsylvania

Winthrop Rockefeller presenting the Freedoms Foundation Educator's Award to Arch Ford in 1964. *Photo courtesy of Economics Arkansas*

presented Commissioner Ford with an award for "exceptional leadership" in bringing about "educational programs which build a better understanding of the American Credo on which our way of life is based." A group of state Supreme Court justices and the national heads of patriotic, veterans, and service club organizations chose the winners from a group of nationwide educators who were nominated by the public. Former president Dwight D. Eisenhower was chairman of the board for the foundation at the time.[74]

Ford was featured in an *Education* article, "Leaders in Education," in May 1963. The article described his leadership experience in education and related some of his beliefs about the future of education. The articles said he was a "strong advocate of broad-purpose federal general aid to education," but that he believed the future of education "lies largely in the leadership potential of state departments of education."[75]

His leadership in the Department of Education also gained him recognition within the state. He was often a graduation speaker at high schools and colleges or a featured speaker at civic clubs, chamber of commerce events, or other civic events. In 1972, John L. Ferguson, a noted Arkansas historian, chose him to serve on the Arkansas Creed Selection Committee. The creed the committee crafted and adopted stated, "I believe in Arkansas as a land of opportunity and promise. I believe in the rich heritage of Arkansas and I honor the men and women who created this heritage. I believe in the youth of Arkansas who will build our future. I am proud of my State. I will uphold its constitution, obey its laws, and work for the good of all its citizens."[76]

Arch Ford Education Building. *Photo courtesy of Ron Beckman*

In a *Nashville News* article published in 1977, Dr. Bessie Moore, director of the Arkansas Council on Economic Education, commented, "Ford's reputation as a man of wisdom extends to nationwide education circles. I've had two U.S. commissioners of education tell me that they don't make any major policy decision without discussing it with Ford. I think people nationally appreciate him more than the home folks do."[77]

Life in the Commissioner's Office

Commissioner Ford conducted his office and himself in a practical, down-to-earth fashion. He rode to work each day in a carpool from Conway that included six employees of the Department of Education. The only time he didn't was when the legislature was in session. Then he might stay over at his son Joe's house. Joe lived in Little Rock and was then a state senator.

He was not one to go out to a restaurant to eat lunch every day.

His wife, Ruby, packed him a lunch in a little lunch box. His usual meal was a two-inch-thick sandwich and a package of peanut-butter crackers. His wife tried to keep him from eating sweets, but he would sometimes sneak down to the coffee shop for a donut. Dorothy Gillam, his administrative assistant, said in an interview that he would try to hide it from her (although she never told his wife).[78]

Dorothy Gillam, who was hired by Commissioner Ford to integrate the Department of Education in 1965, came to work in his office after about four years of working in federal programs. She later became his administrative assistant and still serves in the Commissioner's Office at the Department of Education. In 2015, she was honored for fifty years of service in the department.[79]

Ford was also in the habit of taking a nap after his lunch. He said that a member of the Board of Education who was a doctor had advised him to take a nap every day. He would stretch out on the sofa in his office, and Dorothy had strict orders not to wake him except when his son Joe called or when the afternoon edition of the *Arkansas Democrat* arrived.[80]

Major advancements were made in Arkansas education during the over thirty-seven years Arch Ford was at the Department of Education, which will be detailed in subsequent chapters. His early objectives would be realized, and the quality of Arkansas education would be improved through higher standards and more funding. But he would also have the challenge of guiding Arkansas public schools through the choppy political waters of McCarthyism and desegregation.

Chapter 4: Financing Education in Arkansas: The Perennial Problem

Over the years, finding the financial resources to fund public education in Arkansas has been one of the biggest hurdles toward creating a quality system of education for all children in the state. When Arkansas entered the twentieth century, there were some 5,000 local school districts in the state. This was partly due to the fact that the education initiatives in the nineteenth century had been focused on making schools available to children in all parts of the state. Since children often had to walk to school, one-room schoolhouses had to be placed within a reasonable distance to students. Arch Ford himself, when he started school in the fall of 1912, had to walk a mile each day to get to the two-room academy in Wooster.

The problem that emerged after World War I, however, was that many began to see the need for education beyond the eighth grade, and the existing schools did not have the resources to provide a high school education for their students. Even districts that did have high schools were often so small that they could not receive accreditation. Many students had to do as Arch Ford did—go to a nearby city for high school because their hometowns could not provide further education.

Many felt that the only way to be able to afford high schools for all students in the state was to consolidate the districts so that they could share resources. Several key measures were passed in the late 1920s to try to provide adequate funding for Arkansas schools. Amendment 11 to the Arkansas Constitution, approved in 1926, increased the property tax that a school district could levy from twelve to eighteen mills. Act 28 of 1927 established a state equalization fund, administered by the state Board of Education, to aid poorer districts. Act 156 of 1927 empowered county boards of education to form new school districts within the county or change the boundary lines of existing school districts if the majority of residents wanted to consolidate districts. Act 149 of 1929 allowed for the consolidation of a county's school districts into a single district, with voter approval. These reforms dropped the number of Arkansas school districts from 4,711 to around 1,900 by the mid-1930s.[81]

World War II further crippled Arkansas's inadequate school system as public school teachers left their classrooms to work in defense jobs or left the state entirely for better-paying positions in other states. Many of the male teachers were drafted and had to leave their classrooms to go fight.

Arch Ford at his desk in the Commissioner's Office. *Photo courtesy of Economics Arkansas*

Many schools simply had to close because of the shortage of teachers.

After the war, efforts were renewed to consolidate districts so that efficiencies could be achieved and high school could be provided. Supporters of Initiated Act 1 in 1946 claimed that 100,000 of the state's 406,199 students lived in districts that had no high school at all and 76,000 more lived in districts whose high school was too small to receive accreditation. That meant that 43% of Arkansas students did not have access to a quality high school education.[82]

The act would have dissolved all school districts that had fewer than 350 students and merge them into newly created county districts. Unfortunately, Initiated Act 1 did not pass in 1946 because of fears that local school districts would lose control of their schools. The legislature also made things worse by repealing the *ad valorem* property tax in 1947, which meant that the almost $2 million that had been funding public schools disappeared. Although some state taxes were raised to try to compensate for the loss of revenue, it was not enough.[83]

In 1948, supporters of Initiated Act 1 decided to try again. Changes were made to the 1948 Initiated Act 1 bill to ensure that any decisions of the county school board could be appealed. This time, the act was paired with another school reform, proposed Amendment 40. This amendment to the Arkansas Constitution would remove the existing eighteen mill ceiling on the amount of money local school districts could raise to support the schools. This time, both measures passed with over 60% voting in favor of the changes.[84]

Within a year, the number of school districts in Arkansas dropped from 1,600 in 1948 to 423 in 1949. State Commissioner Ralph Jones said that the passage of Initiated Act 1 and Amendment 40 pointed to "an era of educational advancement in this state that never has been known before." A study done by the Arkansas Legislative Council in 1951 also found the reforms to be "a remarkable achievement and one in which the state can well be proud. It is now possible for all educable children in the state to attend school for 12 years. A high school is within reach of all children. This, in itself, is a notable achievement."[85]

Ford also considered these two reforms to be largely responsible for setting Arkansas on the path to a better education system. In addition, in many interviews, he credited Governor Sid McMath for their passage. "We would never have passed that amendment without the aggressive and enthusiastic support of Sid McMath, who was the Democratic nominee for Governor. The people of Arkansas owe Sid McMath a debt of gratitude."[86]

Equalization of Opportunity

In a 1979 interview after his retirement, Arch Ford addressed the issue of equal access to education as he reflected on his years at the Department of Education. He said, "The central issue in education in our time has been universal access to the schools, for minorities, the poor and the handicapped. That's the thing that has made the difference."[87] A big portion of his time as commissioner would be spent expanding educational opportunities to those who had not previously had equal access.

As the U.S. Supreme Court was considering *Brown v. Board of Education of Topeka* in 1954, Arkansas leaders were looking at what they could do to equalize the school facilities of black and white students in the state. This had been one of Arch Ford's goals when he took the commissioner's job, and it was also on the minds of those on the Arkansas Legislative Council.

In a June 6, 1954, interview shortly after the Court announced its decision, Commissioner Ford said, "If the local districts in heavily populated Negro areas are to maintain substantially the present pattern, Negro schools must be improved in those areas. If this is not done, the next step will be lowering standards of white schools." He hinted that the state may not be able to do it alone and that additional taxes on the local level may be necessary. "We believe that additional funds will be needed in many of the 228 districts having students of both races from both the state and local levels." He said the additional money, which some estimated at about $20 million, would be needed for both the operation of school facilities and the construction of new buildings.[88]

Finding more money to give *all* Arkansas children, regardless of race or geographic location, a quality education became a major theme during Commissioner Ford's tenure. The road to increasing funding for education included more consolidation, more per pupil spending, and higher teacher salaries.

One of the first significant reforms that improved the funding for education was an assessment equalization plan passed by the General Assembly in 1955 that called for a major property reassessment in all counties. In a March 1955 interview, Ford said, "The equalization program will be a painful process but it is a must if we are to solve some of our basic problems. We sincerely hope that the approach which is being made now will prove successful. If it should fail we will have to make a different approach to the same problem. We do not mean to imply that it is our opinion that the state has reached the saturation point so far as state revenues are concerned. We do believe, however, that the time has come when the people at the local level must face up to the assessment problem. Volunteer assessments will no longer do the job in Arkansas."[89]

Another significant improvement in education funding came from the recommendations of the Governor's Advisory Council on Education (GACE), which Governor Orval Faubus set up in 1956. The governor commissioned the group to do a study on what could be done to improve education in the state. In December 1956, the group presented a recommendation for an $18 million project that would increase sales, income, and severance taxes. It proposed a one-cent sales tax that would bring in about $15 million.

GACE also presented a draft for a new school aid formula bill. Dr. Francis G. Cornell of New York, a hired consultant, had drafted the bill. It placed the annual expenditure for each school student at a minimum of $130, which was the average expenditure at that time. The existing minimum was about $40. It was based on the idea of determining a district's ability in sharing school costs with the state. This "ability index" would be based on the county's proportion of the total sales tax collections, vehicle registration fees, gainfully employed workers, and assessed valuation of public utilities.

The bill also enacted penalties by withholding state aid from districts that had not voted at least an eighteen mill tax in the previous fiscal year and had not paid the minimum teachers' salaries required by law. At least 90% of the revenues would go to teachers' salaries, and some of the money would also be used for teacher aides, textbooks and other school supplies, or school buses. "With the additional money, the state could take care of its retarded and exceptional children, as well as things like speech correction, all of which are virtually neglected in most Arkansas schools," said Lonnie Ethridge, president of Arkansas School Boards Association.[90]

The one-cent sales tax was passed by the General Assembly in the 1957 session, but the fight still wasn't over. Alex Washburn, a publisher from Hope, tried to get the tax increase repealed through a referendum. Governor Orval Faubus called GACE together to come up with a plan to fight the referendum. He said if the 3% sales tax was rejected by the people "the schools, the university, the colleges and other essential governmental services will be immediately thrown into chaos." Most of the additional $16 million expected would increase salaries for the state's 14,000 teachers. He further made the point that "education is related to the state's economic well-being."[91]

Arkansas got a real boost in its education funding when Congress passed the National Science Education Act in 1958. Under this act, school districts could match funds with the government for the construction of science classrooms and improvements in science, math, and related scientific studies. It was estimated that this would bring in about $1.6 million a year.[92]

Arkansas would get even more federal funding through the Elementary and Secondary Education Act of 1965, which would provide millions of dollars in aid. When it was announced, Arkansas was told to expect about $21 million through the act, but Commissioner Ford said in an August 1965 interview that this probably would be reduced by 20 to 25% the first year because of amendments to the initial law. He said that the reduction would be only for the first year and would in no way affect the start of the programs in Arkansas. "I doubt that we will be able to make full use of the money we will be allocated in the first year," he said.[93]

The money was made available to districts on a project basis, so the Education Department could withhold approval of programs that did little to enrich the lot of disadvantaged. To qualify for funding, the programs had to focus on students who were disadvantaged as a result of one or more of three factors: they were from low-income families, they were dependent on the state, or they were physically disabled. It was estimated that about 40% of the children probably would get personalized services in the form of eyeglasses, hearing aids, and whatever else was needed to help them in schooling. This also included breakfasts and lunches for children who otherwise would go hungry, clothing, elementary and high school textbooks, and other items that were allowed by the law. The majority of the disadvantaged children were white because white students outnumbered black students in the state. But the percentage of black students who were disadvantaged was about twice that of whites. "We must keep in mind that the poorest part of Arkansas is in the north central part of the state where there are relatively few Negro families," Ford said.[94]

The Arkansas General Assembly took another step in 1965 to ensure more money for education. It passed the Revenue Stabilization Act, which guaranteed the schools a minimum amount of funds for the biennium. The legislature also passed Act 164, which provided public schools with 90% of any surplus above the Stabilization Act commitment and pledged any such increase toward teacher salaries.[95]

By the late 1960s, there began to be more concern about the *distribution* of education funds than the *availability* of funds. Some districts were collecting about $133 million a year in property taxes, and some were able to spend more per pupil than others because of more valuable property being taxed or because of higher millage rates. The state was putting more and more funds into the poorer districts in order to close the gap.

In early 1972, Governor Dale Bumpers set up the Governor's Advisory Committee on School Finance and Property Tax to study the property tax system and school finance so that the committee could be ready with information and recommendations for him and the General Assembly. The committee subsequently recommended that the legislature appropriate an extra $1.5 million to distribute to the poorest school districts to help close the gap.

Lieutenant Governor Bob Riley, chairman of the committee, said the committee recommended that future legislatures follow the precedent and put additional state funds into poor districts. He believed the state still had a great obligation to bring equity to its tax system and its education spending. He thought the assessors needed firmer guidelines for assessing property to relieve them of the political liabilities of their job. He expected that the state could achieve equalization in school finance in five years.[96]

The problem did not resolve itself as Lt. Gov. Riley hoped, however. The amount that Arkansas schools were spending to educate their children in 1976, four years later, varied from $581 to $1,167 per child. Several school districts in Northwest Arkansas were beginning to consider lawsuits because a number of them had been growing rapidly and had not gotten enough state aid to accommodate the growth.

To avoid a lawsuit, Commissioner Ford and Governor David Pryor proposed a bill to the legislature in January 1976 that would require equalized spending within four to eight years. The bill would have directed the Board of Education to propose formulas for distributing state aid as a means of balancing the spending per child. The House of Representatives voted not to introduce the bill.

In a February 1976 interview, Ford prophetically said it would probably take a court order to end the wide disparities in the educational opportunities offered by Arkansas school districts. "I don't think we can look to the legislature to resolve the issue. When it turns down even a procedure for resolving it, then that is a clear indication that the legislature doesn't intend to do anything about it."[97] He said he had decided it was probably unfair to ask the legislature or other elected officials to resolve it. Legislators, he said, are always torn between the competing wishes within the area they represent, with some school districts benefiting and some losing under an equalized spending formula. He added that he did not advocate a lawsuit to force equalized school spending but said, "I'm not expecting any substantial progress on this issue unless and until the present system is successfully challenged in court."[98]

In the February 1976 *Education Newsmagazine* published by the Arkansas Department of Education, Commissioner Ford said that the Arkansas education funding system could probably be attacked on several grounds. He said state aid to schools in Arkansas was distributed partly on the basis of the old system of segregated schools, in which biracial districts operated two sets of schools. Before dual school systems were outlawed, the state weighted its aid to schools to give more money to those that had to administer dual school systems. The dual system was later abolished, but those districts were still receiving the extra financial aid. Also, some of the same districts had significant losses in enrollment, but the present system continued to give them the same amount of aid even though their enrollment had declined.

"Certainly rank discrimination is not 'suitable' nor is a dual system," Ford said in the article. The Arkansas Constitution required the state to maintain "suitable" schools for its children, and yet some districts were not providing that. He gave an example of how the Fifty-Six school district spent $1,716 per pupil per year, with seven pupils attending school in the neighboring Mountain View District. It was spending a large amount of money but still did not get an "A" rating from the Department of Education.[99]

Governor Pryor was becoming increasingly concerned about the amount of state aid the school districts were receiving in proportion to local funding. In an interview a few days after Arch Ford made his remarks, Pryor said that 65% of school budgets were coming from state funds. The percentage of budgets raised by local taxes had been declining a little each year. The state shortly would have to evaluate the whole system of financing the public schools to see whether the trend toward complete state funding of the schools was proper.[100]

The General Assembly would approve a school funding formula bill in 1977. The bill, which originated in Governor Pryor's office, was part of his "Arkansas Plan." The governor proposed a formula that would have changed the distribution of some $71 million of state school aid annually to help poor and fast-growing districts that had been hurt by the old formula. Schools the next year would have been guaranteed only the level of aid they were receiving in 1973–74. The next year, the level would be $71 million higher and all of that would have been divided under the new equalization formula.

The proposal ran into trouble because it would have meant a reduction of state aid for sixty-seven districts and a static level for many others. To get the bill out of the education committee in the Senate, Pryor had to agree to guarantee districts their level of aid in 1975–76. Another amendment was added which allowed a district with a pupil-teacher ratio of greater than 21 to 1 to use part of the state aid earmarked for teacher salary increase the next year to hire additional teachers instead. In the past, 80% of funding had to go to raises and additional personnel could be hired with remaining 20%. For one year, they could use more. A final amendment required a list of those districts which were 90 days delinquent on their mortgage payments.[101]

The Joint Interim Committee on Education appointed an advisory committee in 1977 to develop a plan for overhauling the state's system of financing public education. Dr. Kern Alexander from the

University of Florida and his team of consultants were hired to do a study and make recommendations. Alexander made his report to the Joint Interim Committee on Education in the fall of 1978.

One of the harshest statements he made in the report, now known as the Alexander Report, was that Arkansas students would be better off in the schools of almost any other state. In his recommendations, he said the state government should raise state aid to education by at least $65 million a year to bring funding nearer to the national average. He said that much of the increase should be to raise teachers' salaries to a level that would be competitive with those in surrounding states. The committee also recommended that the state, over two or three years, revise its formula for how it distributes state aid to the schools in order to overcome the disparity in educational programs between rich and poor schools. A final recommendation was that the state should consolidate small school districts to reduce the number of districts from 384 to about 200 and provide state help to districts in building and modernizing schools.[102] Commissioner Ford concurred with most of the report.

According to Jim Wooten, a lifetime board member of Economics Arkansas who was interviewed about Ford's legacy, Ford believed that the best way to equalize funding for education was for the money to follow the child. If a student moved to another district, the dollars spent for education would follow him or her to the new district. Wooten stated that he believed that type of plan would have allowed Arkansas to avoid the *Lakeview* situation that arose later.[103]

During the thirty-seven years Ford served in the Department of Education, the total budget of the department grew exponentially. In 1947–48, when Initiated Act 1 and Amendment 40 were passed, the department had a budget of $38.7 million.[104] In 1978, as Arch Ford retired, the legislature had appropriated $287.9 million for the 1978–79 Department of Education budget, and $310.6 million was appropriated for 1979–80.[105] Arkansas's system of education still ranked near the bottom in teachers' salaries and per-pupil expenditures, but it had made great advances.

In 1960, after a dispute with the National Education Association over conflicting per-pupil expenditures that had been reported, Commissioner Ford said in an interview that Arkansas ranked among the first five of the fifty states in support of education in proportion to its ability to pay. "The amount of money spent on education in proportion to the earnings of the people is the real yardstick of the interest of the people in their schools." He said that he was not arguing that states and local communities were doing all they could for education. "Quite the contrary is true in all parts of the nation. We simply must recognize that this is the last half of the 20th century and that education is important."

In the interview, Ford also quoted from a 1954 book by Harry S. Ashmore, former executive editor of the *Arkansas Gazette*, in which he said that Arkansas was ranked ninth in the nation in its effort to support public education in proportion to ability to pay as of 1954. In a 1960 *Gazette* article, Ford said, "Since 1954, Arkansas has increased its sales tax 50%, adjusted the income tax upward, and has completed an equalization of assessments program which resulted in substantial increases. Millage reductions for the support of schools have, on the average, been nominal. While other states have increased their effort to support public education, it is a known fact that most states have not made a triple increase as is true in Arkansas....I believe it is safe to assert that Arkansas now ranks among the first five of the 50 states in support of education in proportion to ability to pay."[106]

Chapter 5: Improving the Quality of Arkansas Education

I nitiated Act 1 of 1948 was a giant step toward improving the education of Arkansas students because it reduced the number of school districts in the state, making a high school education possible for all students. Amendment 40 of 1948, which took the ceiling off property tax rates, plus property value reassessment, gave the school districts more money to improve the quality of the education that was offered. Additional financial assistance from sales tax revenue and from federal programs also allowed local school districts to improve their educational systems.

But inadequate financing was not the only weakness in the state's school districts. Many districts were running terms of only five or six months with a split summer term to accommodate the farming families. There was a great scarcity of teachers, so many of the schools had one-room–one-teacher classrooms. Because of the shortage, the standards were pretty low when districts hired teachers.

In 1950-51, Department of Education records showed that there were 255 teachers in Arkansas with fewer than 30 hours of college degree work; 1,238 with fewer than 60 hours; 1,913 with fewer than 90 hours; and 2,959 with 90 or more hours but not a degree. Out of 14,120 teachers in Arkansas, there were only 6,597 with a bachelor's degree; 1,155 with a master's degree; and three with a doctorate.[107] Efforts would be made during Arch Ford's tenure as commissioner of the Department of Education to improve the quality of education in Arkansas schools by improving the quality of teachers, by further consolidation, and, finally, by making improvements in the curriculum.

Improving the Quality of Teachers

When Arch Ford became commissioner in 1953, the law still required only 30 hours of training or one year of college in order to get a standard teaching certificate. A survey taken in that year revealed that 650 or 8.4% of the 7,757 classroom teachers still lacked two years of college training. The greatest percentage of these teachers could be found in the Delta region or in the small mountain districts of Northwest Arkansas. The survey also showed that Arkansas had lost 22% of its teachers the previous year through teachers moving out of state for better-paying positions, getting married, or quitting the profession. This caused an even more severe scarcity of qualified teachers in the state.[108]

In 1954, the state Board of Education put out a statement that it would no longer issue teaching permits to those with fewer than 60 hours of college training. This had been recommended by educators to upgrade the level of teaching in the state. Unfortunately, the Arkansas House of Representatives passed a bill that overruled the board and legalized the 30-hour permits. The bill's sponsors said that some districts were not able to hire teachers with that level of education. State officials agreed to submit a new regulation to the Board of Education, and the Senate Education Committee let the bill die in committee.

The new regulation was sent to the board in June 1955. School districts could employ, when necessary, teachers with only 30 hours of college training, but the board would allow 30-hour permits for one year only. The district superintendent had to submit evidence that no applicants with higher qualifications were available in order to get the waiver. The 60-hour requirement would then go into effect June 1956.[109]

Meanwhile, Governor Orval Faubus commissioned his Governor's Advisory Council on Education (GACE) to conduct a two-year study on how to improve the quality of teaching services in Arkansas. John G. Rye of Russellville, a GACE member and vice-chairman of the state Board of Education, said in his outline for the study that other states had outdone Arkansas in enforcing standards for teaching services. He said Arkansas was the only state certifying high school teachers on less than a bachelor's degree.

"This situation has placed the state in a tragically handicapped position in the competition for the short supply of qualified teachers; and with higher standards in surrounding states, Arkansas will inevitably become the dumping grounds for the teacher cast-offs from other states, unless remedial actions are immediately taken, and vigorously," Rye said. He went on to say that the people of Arkansas had indicated that they wanted a better education for their children, and steps had to be taken by the teaching profession with the assistance of their communities.[110]

Commissioner Ford reported in March 1959 that progress had been made in improving the qualifications of classroom teachers. He reported that in 1947–48 there were 1,579 teachers with less than two years of college, but in 1957–58 there were only 151 who had less than two years of college. He also reported that there were only 1,200 teachers (8.6%) out of the 13,933 teachers employed in Arkansas schools who had fewer than 90 hours of college education.[111]

In 1960, the Arkansas Department of Education ramped up its efforts to raise the quality of teachers. A State Advisory Council on Teacher Education and Certification, made up of fifty educators, was commissioned to do a study and make recommendations. The council reported that there were 3,500 out of the 14,200 Arkansas teachers who did not yet have a degree. They recommended a five-year plan to reduce this number. Also, beginning July 1, 1960, all new teachers hired would have to have a degree from an accredited college or university; thirteen of the fifteen colleges with teacher training programs were accredited at that time. The plan included making sure that all of these colleges would be accredited within the five-year period.

Under the new regulations, current teachers would need to get their degree or find employment elsewhere. They would have five years to complete their degree by taking classes during summer vacations. All of these teachers would have to show that had achieved a 120-hour program of balanced study. The plan called for districts to be allowed to renew the contracts for one year if the teacher had added six semester hours or more of work during the year. Unqualified teachers near retirement would be "treated gently," and retirement laws would be relaxed so these teachers could still retire.[112]

A later report by the State Education Study Commission specified that non-degree teachers with 90 or more semester hours had to earn an average of six semester hours a year until their degrees were earned but that those with fewer than 90 hours would be required to earn nine to twelve hours a year. The report went on to say, "When these new certification standards become fully effective, Arkansas will be well on the road to a profession of teaching and potential quality of scholarship in all our classrooms and in all teaching fields."[113]

Commissioner Ford, in an article he wrote for the *Arkansas Democrat* in early 1963, reported that, since 1960–61, a total of 901 teachers had secured degrees. This means that 88% of the teachers in Arkansas had degrees.[114] That year, the state Board of Education began to consider raising the standards even further. Ford proposed that the board begin to study the possibility of requiring that secondary teachers obtain a college degree in an academic subject rather than one in education methodology. "I think a teacher ought to have an education. It's important that she know what to teach as well as how to teach," he said.[115]

At a later meeting that year, the board also approved a plan to issue master's certificates to elementary and secondary teachers who earned master's degrees. This was done to provide an extra measure of professional recognition for the teachers.[116]

Reports were made periodically over the next several years on the progress of improving the education of teachers. In 1966, a state survey showed that 752 (4.4%) out of 18,070 teachers still lacked a college degree. There were now 13,788 with a bachelor's degree; 3,522 with a master's degree, and eight with a doctorate.[117] In 1967, it was reported that 97% of all teachers now had bachelor's degrees and 21% had a master's degree.[118] In 1970, it was reported that almost 99% of the 19,532 teachers had a bachelor's degree, while 4,056 had achieved a master's degree. Over 12% had doctorates and 12% had certificates of advanced study.[119]

Commissioner Ford then began a campaign to improve the quality of education that the teachers were receiving. Beginning in September 1972, new standards were implemented by the state Board of Education for teacher certification. The standards offered a variety of certificates for relatively new teaching areas and prescribed courses of study that had to be taken to qualify for the certificates. Special certificates would be issued for elementary guidance counselors, elementary physical education teachers, elementary reading teachers, elementary librarians and media specialists, health education teachers, journalism teachers, curriculum specialists, and instructional supervisors. Those wishing to have a business education certification would now have to take more sophisticated business courses such as economics and business law. Certification in foreign language would require six hours in functional language skills. Before these new standards were implemented, teachers could be certified in a variety of courses such as literature of a foreign country, which did not train the teacher in the actual skills of the language.

Rigor was added to the academic programs. Those seeking a math certificate would now have to have 21 semester hours of math courses instead of 18, and specific courses would be required. More requirements for specific courses were written into the social science standards. A course in earth science would be required for a certificate in general science. A person with a special education certification would have to have training in precisely the type of special education class to which he or she would be assigned. Secondary school principals would also be required to have 15 semester hours above their master's degree.[120]

Improving Teacher Salaries

One final thing helped Arkansas improve the quality of teachers during this time. It was nearly impossible to hire and keep teachers if they were not paid an adequate salary. The teachers in Arkansas would not have cooperated with the higher standards being imposed on them if there had not also been a greater effort to improve their salaries at the same time. Commissioner Ford, the governor, and many legislators campaigned tirelessly during this time to improve the salaries of Arkansas teachers.

The average teacher's salary in the 1947-48 school year in Arkansas was $1,548 a year. In 1953, the General Assembly passed the Minimum School Budget Law, which would provide about $600,000 more a year for teachers' salaries. It also required that school districts spend 75% of their new revenues on teachers' salaries.[121] The legislature budgeted raises for the next several years and, by 1957-58, the average teacher's salary had doubled to an annual salary of $3,153.[122] Commissioner Ford was so adamant about teacher raises that he said in 1955 that he would not accept a raise unless teachers also got one. His salary was $8,400 a year, and Senator Guy "Mutt" Jones had suggested it be raised to $10,000.[123]

By 1967-68, the average teacher's salary had risen to $5,669 a year, and it had risen to $9,974 a year by 1975-76.[124] During the next biennium, Governor David Pryor and the Arkansas General

Assembly agreed to raise teachers' salaries by an average of $600 a year.[125] Arkansas salaries were still very low compared to the rest of the fifty states, but the raises did help keep enough teachers in the state so that the quality of education improved.

In a 1979 interview after his retirement, Arch Ford reflected on the gains that were made by Arkansas teachers and said, "It's going to wind up that teaching will be a pretty good job in this state."[126]

More Consolidation to Improve Quality

One of the most popular suggestions for improving the quality of education in Arkansas was to consolidate more districts and close the schools that could not provide a quality education for their students. Arch Ford favored consolidation as a way to improve the schools, but he preferred to allow local districts to come to their own conclusions and consolidate on their own.[127]

In 1956, Governor Faubus's advisory council, GACE, recommended that reorganization take place to eliminate small and inefficient school districts. GACE's hired consultant recommended that any school with a high school enrollment under 100 be denied any new state funds if it failed to consolidate on the recommendations of the county Board of Education and approval of the state Board of Education. There were seventy-five high schools in the state at the time with enrollments of fewer than 100.

Although a proponent of consolidation, Arch Ford opposed this plan because he feared it would cause trouble in dual school systems in which there were separate black and white schools. He thought the proposal had merit but said that "it is a matter of timing and I don't think the legislature will buy it." He also said, "I do not believe in penalizing children by withholding money from a district in which they happen to live."[128]

In 1963, the Senate proposed that each county create a commission to study the adequacy of the educational program and propose a plan of school district consolidation. Three members from each school board in the county and three members from the county Board of Education would be on each commission. The commissions would be required to prepare a reorganization plan and submit it to the state Department of Education by October 1, 1964.

Under this plan, each county would be able to make an honest appraisal according to state and national standards. Each district would have to show that it could provide an adequate education program for all twelve grades. The state Department of Education would assist in the preparation of the plans when requested, and it had to approve them. Reorganization would not go into effect unless the voters in the district approved. Senator Clarence Bell, sponsor of the bill and superintendent of Parkin School District, said that many children were attending small, substandard schools that were costly to operate. They were being deprived of educational opportunities, and taxpayers were not getting an adequate return on their investment.[129]

Commissioner Ford, in a meeting with school administrators that year, said that one of the trends he saw in Arkansas education was more local interest in developing better schools. This often led to a reexamination of programs in school districts, with the finding that better programs could result through consolidation of small districts into larger ones.[130]

Again in 1964, Arch Ford suggested that public school education in the state could be improved almost overnight by the closing of about 100 high schools that were "weak" and were diluting the educational program. He said that a self-analysis school program inaugurated by him would assess the situation of these districts. He proposed an alternative to mandatory school district consolidation by merging districts unable to finance modern educational programs with those that could and suggested the state pay a tuition grant and extra transportation costs as an incentive. In this interview, he said he hoped to have recommendations for the 1965 General Assembly after a study was done by the Advisory Council on Public Elementary and Secondary Education, which was set up as a permanent council in 1963.[131]

Faced with the threat of statewide forced consolidation, the rural forces in the legislature passed Act 21 in 1965. But that did not keep the Arkansas Education Association (AEA) from taking up the fight for consolidation in 1966. In its argument for consolidation, it presented as evidence the lack of curricular offerings and the cost of small schools. It sponsored Initiated Act No. 1, which would have dissolved all districts with fewer than 400 students by June 1, 1967; a total of 132 districts would have been eliminated. The Arkansas Rural Education Association, which had organized in early 1966, fought the consolidation act. It attacked the AEA by spending $20,000 for newspaper ads, bumper stickers, and literature. All of the gubernatorial candidates opposed consolidation. Initiated Act No. 1 was defeated by a large margin.[132]

Finally, in 1969, Arch Ford and his son, Senator Joe Ford, drafted a bill that would become known as the Quality Education Act. It required school districts to meet state standards by the end of 1979 or face consolidation. Senator Clarence E. Bell of Parkin and Senator Joe Ford of Little Rock sponsored the bill in the Senate.[133] The act required all schools to obtain an "A" rating by the state Department of Education by 1979. Districts that did not achieve the rating would be annexed by an adjoining district. There were about 110 districts that would have to comply with the standards to avoid annexation. It was aimed at upgrading the quality of education in many small districts that had poor curricula. It was based on the recommendations of the Advisory Council on Public Elementary and Secondary Education.[134]

In a January 1979 interview after his retirement, Ford said that he considered the Quality Education Act to be one of his greatest accomplishments during his tenure as commissioner. He said that the 1979 deadline was approaching for the schools to meet the standards, and he expected that fifteen to twenty schools would have to consolidate. He felt that the Quality Education Act was also valuable in forcing many other districts to improve their programs. He said it would be desirable to eliminate about seventy-five school districts that were too small to be efficient but that he did not think it was the overriding issue in education. "We have only 7 or 8 percent of our students in small districts. It would be desirable. It would help those kids and it would make it easier to administer school aid equitably and uniformly," he said.

He also still believed that all school district consolidation had to come about as a result of the vote of the people in the district rather than as a result of actions by the legislature. "The legislature has never taken a hold of the school district situation and I don't anticipate that it will. It might if the governor insisted on it, but I doubt if he'll do it. It creates bitter opposition without gaining you much support, and people who are elected governor are not inclined to welcome those kinds of issues."[135]

Extending the School Term

As the financial situation of school districts improved and the quality of education rose, the remnants of the old school systems began to fade away. All schools in the state were able to run a nine-month term by the 1957-58 school year.[136] However, there were still split terms in 1961 in about thirty districts serving 500 students. These districts were mostly in the cotton-growing areas of eastern Arkansas. But that was almost half of what existed in 1960.

In a 1961 interview, Commissioner Ford said, "The split term school is on the way out. I think that every large school district has discontinued these terms." Ford said that farm mechanization and a changing farm economy were primarily the reasons for the decline of split term schools and that the state Board of Education had urged districts to abandon split terms. "For one thing, the students and the faculty are subjected to hot and humid weather which is not good for teaching. There also is a break in faculty personnel. Some districts are forced to pick up teachers from the larger districts who want to earn some extra money. The ties between these teachers and the students are not as strong as those between the students and their regular teachers." He explained that the state did not want to force local districts to abandon the program, because such a change could dislocate a community economy. The better course had been to let each community see that the split term was not beneficial and better discarded with the minimum of delay.[137]

By 1969, there were no more districts running a split term.

Improving Curriculum

The Soviet launching of Sputnik caused Arkansas, and most other states, to reexamine the curriculum it was offering students in the public schools. In December 1957, the Arkansas Advisory Council on Secondary Education was formally organized. Hal Robbins was named the permanent chairman over a group of eighty-five teachers, superintendents, and other representatives from the AEA and the state Department of Education. The objectives of the group were to clarify the basic philosophies of secondary education, develop public information programs to further the understanding of secondary-education goals, and develop ways to enrich the educational experience at the secondary level.[138]

In January 1958, this study of the high school curriculum in the state was conducted. The council would subsequently recommend that more mathematics and science be offered. It also recommended that agriculture and home economics should be de-emphasized.[139] Ford cautioned that schools should not let this current push for more science and math dim "the true goals" of schools. "We cannot let our school systems become brain-washing institutions swaying to the will of the central government. Schools must continue to improve programs in line with our basic belief in the freedom and dignity of the individual."[140] The National Defense Education Act, however, would bring federal money to help school districts improve the mathematics, science, and foreign language curriculum in the high schools. Even years later, it is still debated as to whether this trend unwittingly lessened the importance of other subjects like history and civics.

One of the trends in education that Commissioner Ford was pleased to see in 1958 was that parents and the general public were beginning to be more interested in what their children were learning at school. Parents still wanted to make sure their children were taught the "fundamentals" like reading, writing, mathematics, and science. In the past there had been a general focus on getting a high school diploma, but an emphasis on college preparation was emerging. Ford made note of the fact that schools needed to strengthen their course offerings. He said that fewer science courses were being offered than were offered twenty years earlier. He also thought more attention should be given to the "gifted" students who were "loafing." He felt those students should be given a "more challenging study routine."[141]

In 1963, the permanent Advisory Council on Elementary and Secondary Education was established by the state legislature. Its job was to evaluate all of the curriculum and programs in the public schools and present a plan of improvement to the legislature in the upcoming legislative session.[142]

Advancing Education in Arkansas

In 1977, the Arkansas General Assembly passed a law that required the state Board of Education to adopt a statement of general goals for public education. The board adopted the following set of goals at its November 1977 meeting:[143]

• Provide students with the necessary basic reading and mathematics skills for them to function at their maximum potential, develop skills to enable students to function effectively in dealing with problem-solving situations, and develop skills to enable students to effectively use all modes of expression, including listening.

• Provide every student with knowledge of career options and a respect for the dignity of work with the opportunity to develop a job-entry level skill and give every student an understanding of economic concepts and how they relate to management of time, money, and personal resources.

• Foster creativity through the arts and develop specific learning skills, including critical thinking, decision making, and the use of the scientific method to facilitate independent life-long learning.

• Help students become responsible and humane citizens through understanding government and the need for individual participation; develop a sense of personal and civic responsibility; promote an appreciation for natural, social, political, and economic heritage; promote an understanding of world cultures; and develop self-discipline, moral values, and a respect for the rights and property of others, including those who think and act differently.

• Help students maintain healthful living by promoting good physical and mental health, developing the capacity for creative use of leisure time, and developing positive and realistic self-concepts and family living skills.

The law also required the board to adopt "minimum performance educational goals for various grades and subject areas." The Department of Education, working with classroom teachers, developed minimum performance goals and standards in reading, writing, and mathematics for first-, third-, and sixth-grade students in the winter of 1977–78. These goals and standards were adopted by the state Board of Education in March 1978.

The goals were general objectives, and the standards were specific steps for measuring the achievement of the goals. Two retired supervisors in the department were hired as consultants to assist in the development of the goals and standards. The goals and standards were reviewed by a committee of elementary teachers before being presented to the board for approval.[144]

Many voiced concerns about what this meant, and Ford said he shared some of their concerns. He said that the board would make it clear to local school officials that the minimum standards were to be guidelines for the teachers and were not to be applied in the schools as minimum standards for passing. There was also some talk at the time about developing tests to make sure the standards were being taught. Legislation to require testing was introduced in the 1977 legislative session, but education groups were successful in blocking it.[145]

Some legislators intended for the next step to be the establishment of minimum standards for graduation from high school. Ford said that such a movement was declining both nationally and in Arkansas. "That's running its course in this state. I don't think the legislature is about to do it," Ford said.[146]

Today, we know that the movement did not run its course nationally or in the state. There are grade and subject goals and standards for every grade level. There are core requirements for graduation from Arkansas's high schools. There is also standardized testing that is used to measure whether a school district is meeting educational goals.

Arkansas made tremendous leaps in its education system during Commissioner Ford's tenure. In a 1975 speech to the South Arkansas Development Council, Ford reflected on the state of education in Arkansas. "What we have done in education is almost unbelievable," he said, pointing out that most of the progress in Arkansas education had come about in the previous twenty-five years. He said, "The South did not generally embark in public education until after the

Civil War. Public education in the South is really only about 100 years old, but we have made tremendous progress."[147]

He realized that not everyone had the same opinion about Arkansas's public schools. In a 1977 interview, he said, "The public school system here is the envy of the whole world, and everybody ought to be proud of their public schools, but they're not. This doesn't mean that there aren't a lot of improvements to be made." Among the improvements he saw that needed to be made were a "return to those elusive and nebulous 'basics' that include respect for elders, good manners, consideration of others, and empathy for all the finer things in our culture. Back in the old days, children were taught these things in the home, but now there's no one there when they get there."[148] He did have a few words for the critics. He said, "I believe a person ought to be FOR something. I have little time for faultfinders."[149]

Dealing with Discipline

In his last few years as commissioner, Ford tried to get some sort of state-wide discipline plan in place. He thought discipline was the number-one problem facing schools at this time.[150] In early 1975, the state School Boards Association and members of the state Department of Education drafted a bill that would set statewide guidelines for discipline.[151] The 1975 legislature created the Commission on Pupil Discipline to develop a set of guidelines that could serve as a model to school districts. The commission members, however, were dissatisfied with the product because the legislature did not provide them with enough funding to do a more comprehensive report.[152]

One of the biggest school discipline issues in the mid-1970s dealt with corporal punishment. In 1977, the U.S. Supreme Court ruled in *Ingraham v. Wright* that the U.S. Constitution's prohibition of "cruel and unusual punishment" did not apply to corporal punishment. The debate about whether it was cruel to students continued anyway, and paddling was replaced by other methods of discipline in most schools by the 1990s. Many proponents of corporal punishment believed that the lack of corporal punishment made discipline problems in the school even worse.

Chapter 6: Desegregating Arkansas's Public Schools

A rkansans were contemplating the impact that the U.S. Supreme Court's decision in *Brown v. Board of Education of Topeka* in 1954 regarding "separate but equal" school facilities might have on their state long before the Court finally handed down its decision. In December 1953, the state Board of Education appointed a three-member committee to evaluate the inequalities in education in Arkansas and to submit in January 1954 a "calm and sensible" statement for local school districts on segregation and equalization.

Marvin Bird, chairman of the board, said the principal reason for the board's action was to "advise the people and reassure them." He further explained, "We want to quiet their feelings on this segregation matter." The chairman told members of the board that he did not think that the pending suits before the Supreme Court constituted a serious threat to education in Arkansas, as many believed. Even granting that segregation might be abolished, he felt that southern states would be given ample time to carry out such on the state level. It did not mean that "overnight Arkansas would have to abolish its present school system."[153]

Assisting the three board members in an advisory capacity were Sam Dickinson, editorial writer with the *Arkansas Democrat*; Harry Ashmore, executive editor of the *Arkansas Gazette*; Dr. Lawrence Davis, president of Arkansas AM&N College in Pine Bluff; Commissioner Arch Ford; and Dr. Ed McCuistion, head of the Division on Negro Education for the Department of Education.

When the Supreme Court handed down its ruling in May 1954, Arch Ford was not surprised by or opposed to the decision. In a 1968 interview, he explained his reaction to the Court decision: "I was expecting the decision, but not a unanimous decision. I had thought it would be divided. There were three Southerners on the Court at the time." The reaction among most Arkansans was shock, he recalled. "Most people in Arkansas I think it's fair to say, were opposed to that decision."[154]

In that same 1968 interview, Ford remembered that he had first encountered discrimination when he left Faulkner County in the seventh grade to attend school for a year in Pawnee, Oklahoma. "For the first time, I woke up to what discrimination was, as applied to the Indian," Ford said. In his opinion, African Americans had been slaves so long that, after their emancipation and after the Civil War, "people didn't take the Negro too seriously and provide an educational opportunity for him." The result was that African Americans' second-class status was taken for granted and the "idea of individual dignity did not take hold in this country."[155]

Ford said the doctrine of "separate but equal" education never had been a reality and never could have been a reality, primarily because local tax structures, "power structures," and control of the public schools were all in the hands of whites who were not conditioned to do much thinking about African Americans' educational problems. "The degree to which a minority differs in appearance from the majority has quite a lot to do with the degree of discrimination," Ford said.[156]

Despite his personal beliefs, Commissioner Ford knew that there were many in Arkansas who did not feel the same way he did. Therefore, he advocated a state policy of leaving desegregation up to the local school districts and their patrons. He felt it was best to let the local districts initiate the integration of their schools when the time was right.

Governor Francis Cherry and the state Board of Education issued joint statements about a month after the Supreme Court decision was handed down. In general, the policies stated that immediate desegregation of Arkansas's public schools would be "premature"; any definite decisions as to what path Arkansas would take in either abolishing or maintaining segregation would have to await further instructions from the Supreme Court; and school boards on the local level should work toward improving schools and educational opportunities for both black students and white students.[157] In his statement, Governor Cherry was emphatic that Arkansas had no intention of disregarding the Supreme Court decision. "Immediately following the opinion of the Supreme Court concerning segregation in public schools, I suggested that we face the situation calmly. I further stated that we would abide by the law. I reaffirm that statement."[158]

To move toward equalization of school facilities, the state Board of Education, for the first time, announced a policy of accreditation of schools on a district-wide basis. This meant that the district would be evaluated on all of its schools rather than on separate schools. Thus, districts that had inferior schools for African Americans but good schools for white students might suffer a lower rating unless the African American schools were improved. This policy would be implemented on a district-by-district basis over the next three years.[159]

In what was reported as the first public speech made by a state official after the Supreme Court decision was announced, Commissioner Ford said that it was his opinion that "there can be no general state-wide pattern of integration between white and black students at this time." Speaking to the Little Rock Rotary Club, he said the attitudes of the people concerning the issue were important. "We will continue to have segregation unless and until the people at the local level are willing to accept integration," he said.

He also said that it was his belief that the majority of African Americans did not seek immediate integration in public schools, but "all want the legal aspects removed." He thought that "there is no difference of opinion among Negro people. I believe that most Negroes want the integration process to come in an orderly and systematic manner."[160] In regard to the speed of integration, he said, "In my opinion, integration will come in some communities within a relatively short period of time. In others it will perhaps be many years. I believe that most of the Negro leadership in Arkansas wants a gradual process which would take a good many years to accomplish."[161]

Ford also stated that, in his opinion, the problems facing African Americans in Arkansas were largely economic but that education was related to the problems. He believed that one of the most significant reasons for the desire of African Americans to improve their educational opportunities was the strong urge to improve their economic status. "The intelligent Negro knows that economic improvement will come as a result of better opportunities for his children." He added that African Americans "probably realized the economic advantages resulting from a good education better than many white people."[162]

When the U.S. Supreme Court handed down its second *Brown* decision in 1955 after considering schools' arguments requesting relief concerning the task of desegregation, the issue of desegregation was remanded back to the individual school districts and the lower federal courts of each state. Going along with the main points that Arkansas attorney general T. J. Gentry had pleaded before the Court, the Court specified that local conditions be considered in achieving integration and that the transition be policed by the lower federal courts.[163]

The Court did not establish a deadline for completing integration but said it should be accomplished with "all deliberate speed." It indicated that the only districts that might be taken to court were those who did not show "good faith" in accomplishing integration within a reasonable time. No one ventured a definition of "reasonable," and no one predicted when integration in Arkansas would be accomplished. Commissioner Ford issued a joint statement with Forrest Rozzell, president of the Arkansas Education Association, declaring that professional educators would observe the law.[164]

Little Rock Central High School

By the time the U.S. Supreme Court handed down its 1955 decision, Arkansas had a new governor. Orval Faubus was elected governor of Arkansas in November 1955. Even though he served six terms, from 1955 to 1967, and accomplished many things as governor, Orval Faubus is still mainly remembered for his actions during the desegregation of Little Rock Central High School.

Arch Ford and Governor Orval Faubus. *Photo courtesy of Arch Ford Collection, UA Special Collections*

As the Little Rock School District began making plans to desegregate its schools, opposition developed in the form of the Capital Citizens' Council and the Mothers' League of Central High School. Tensions mounted as the 1957–58 school year approached. Both segregationists and school district officials launched a letter-writing campaign for Governor Faubus to intervene in order to prevent the violence that was predicted if desegregation proceeded at Little Rock Central High School. Faubus asked the Department of Justice's civil rights division for assistance in keeping order and was told that the federal government could not help.

The weekend before Little Rock Central was scheduled to open for the fall semester of 1957, Faubus called meetings of about thirty-five of his close advisers and heads of the departments. Meetings were held on both Friday and Saturday. Arch Ford, in a 1968 interview, recalled what happened at those meetings. In the first meeting, which lasted about an hour, Faubus told the group he was considering calling out the state's National Guard to "prevent bloodshed and violence," in much the same terms he later used to justify his action publicly. The governor did not mention the issues of integration or segregation as such, Ford said. He recalled that Faubus was extremely nervous during the meeting. The governor asked the group for advice but received conflicting advice from those present at the meeting. Ford and many others attending were inclined to wait and see what happened. On Saturday, when the group reconvened, Ford recalled that Faubus seemed to be much calmer, so Ford assumed that he had arrived at a decision. However, Faubus did not tell them his decision. They did not know until Faubus announced on Sunday that he had decided to call out the Arkansas National Guard to prevent violence at Central (although it actually turned the black students away).[165] The rest, as they say, is history. Most Arkansans were not proud of what happened.

In December 1957, the state Board of Education considered launching a clinical study on integration to see what could be done to "avoid another Little Rock Central." Four educational organizations had submitted the proposal to the board in November for consideration. The study would call on experts in the fields of sociology and psychology to try to find out how to achieve peaceful integration.

Forrest Rozzell, president of the Arkansas Education Association, said that the study would take a minimum of six months and possibly a year. In his statement to the board, he explained the need for the study. "Since the Civil War, we have had a stable relationship between the races and that has been removed. We need a study of the situation, an analysis of what happened and what it has done to relationships among people." He added that as educators, "we cannot conceive that there is not an answer to this problem, even though we can't see what it is."[166]

Joshua K. Shepherd of Little Rock, vice-chairman of the Governor's Advisory Council on Education (GACE), responded to this proposal by saying the experience of Little Rock had demonstrated that some things cannot be forced on people until they are properly adjusted to accept them.[167] As a result of the Little Rock experience, integration would not be "forced." It would take another act by the federal government to accomplish integration in Arkansas.

Elementary and Secondary Education Act (ESEA)

In the fall of 1962, it was reported that there were 249 African American students attending desegregated schools. (That was compared to 152 students the previous year.) Of the 228 districts that had both black and white students, twelve of the districts were integrated in some or all of their classes—two more than had been desegregated in the previous year.[168]

In 1965, Congress passed the Elementary and Secondary Education Act (ESEA) as part of President Lyndon Johnson's War on Poverty program. This would provide millions of dollars in federal funding for improving education. But in order to receive those funds, states and districts had to agree to comply with the new Civil Rights Act of 1964 that outlawed discrimination. Districts had to submit a desegregation plan to be approved by the state Department of Education and the federal Office of Education. State agencies, such as the Department of Education, also had to desegregate in order to be allowed to administer the disbursement of federal funds.

Commissioner Ford was called to testify before the U.S. House of Representatives subcommittee on education in 1963. It was holding hearings on the elementary and secondary education bill. He told the committee that he opposed federal aid to public schools that was tied to mandatory desegregation. He said he was against the Powell Amendment, a rider that would require desegregation in order for schools to receive the federal funds. He said he believed that such a requirement would deny equal opportunities to all children. There was a fiery exchange between Ford and several legislators. Representative Hugh L. Carey, a Democrat from New York, even asked Ford to supply a record of desegregation in Arkansas since 1954.[169]

Ford and many Arkansans were fearful that forced desegregation would derail the educational progress that had already been made in Arkansas. He testified that Arkansas had made substantial progress in education since World War II. The state had increased its school budget by 300% and the local districts had increased their budgets by 400%. He also said that nearly $15 million was now being spent annually on new schoolhouse construction in Arkansas. "The attitude of the public in Arkansas toward education has changed—materially—in recent years," he explained. "The public is aware as never before that we need better schools. Parents of all economic levels realize that if their children are to have a fair chance to succeed they must have educational opportunities in keeping with the present and future needs."[170]

Ford did endorse a provision of the bill calling for individual state surveys to determine needs among public and private schools, saying it would provide a reasonable approach to the separation-of-church-and-state issue. "The determination of the use of funds would be made by the states, which is the most feasible way in the absence of a court decision of resolving this highly controversial issue."[171]

Congress passed ESEA and did require that school districts submit a desegregation plan to the state Department of Education and to the Office of Education in order to receive federal monies from this program. Just as he had indicated earlier, Ford determined that he would follow the law.

The Civil Rights Act included two means of requiring desegregation. One was the loss of federal aid for failure to comply. Title VI of the Civil Rights Act dealt with discrimination in any federally assisted program. The other was giving the Justice Department the authority to file suit to end discrimination. Any school district that wanted the federal funds provided under ESEA or any other federal program had to file a desegregation plan to get the funding.[172]

Desegregation of the Arkansas Department of Education

In order for the state Department of Education to administer the federal programs, the department and all its associated agencies would have to be desegregated. On June 1, 1965, Commissioner Ford hired an African American woman, Dorothy Mae McKinstry (later Gillam), as a secretary in the School Lunch and Milk Division. The department had three African American employees at the time, but they worked exclusively in related school programs related to black students.[173]

Gillam related in a recent interview that Commissioner Ford had the doors of the bathrooms painted over before she came to work so that they would no longer say "colored." The bathrooms on the bottom floor of the education building were for women and had been designated as "colored" and "white." Ford had the doors painted again and again over the years when the paint faded. Eventually the custodian hung signs over the words so he would not have to repaint the doors. The old signs were still evident until the bathrooms were remodeled a few years ago.[174]

The women she worked with gave her a hard time, and she finally submitted her resignation to her supervisor.[175] Ford called her into his office and told her he was not accepting her resignation. He offered to transfer her to the federal programs office housed in west Little Rock. In 1969, he transferred her to his office as an executive secretary. She later became administrative assistant in the commissioner's office and is still there, working for Commissioner Johnny Key as an administrative analyst.[176] She recently was honored for fifty years of service with the Department of Education.

The Path to Peaceful Integration

A December 1965 *Memphis Commercial Appeal* article said that the path to peaceful integration in Arkansas was paved by Commissioner Arch Ford. On April 1, 1965, Ford had brought U.S. Deputy Commissioner of Education, Wayne O. Reed, to Little Rock for a mass meeting of school board members and superintendents to talk about desegregation. Dr. Reed stayed until 1 a.m. answering school board members' questions.[177]

By the end of 1965, a total of 409 districts in Arkansas had submitted desegregation pans and had peacefully integrated. Arkansas led the entire South—73% of the districts with both black and white students had integrated compared to Louisiana, which had only integrated 13% of its schools. Mississippi had integrated only 21% of its schools, while Alabama had integrated only 51%. No one wanted a repeat of the situation at Little Rock Central. Even Governor Faubus stayed out of it. The small daily and weekly newspapers in Arkansas supported integration efforts. There were few disturbances and they were minor. Arkansas got the federal ESEA money: $6 million of the $21 million that had been allotted had been sent to local schools.[178]

A January 1966 *Arkansas Gazette* article reported that only five Arkansas districts had failed to file a desegregation plan with the Office of Education. The desegregation plans varied from district to district, but most required the desegregation of four grades per year in order to complete integration. Nearly all used the "freedom of choice" plan, which said no actual desegregation would take place unless African American students applied for admission to white schools and were accepted.[179] Thirty-seven districts that had approved plans did not have any black students apply to be admitted in 1966, but there were 6,217 black students out of the 110,755 black students in the state who were in integrated schools in one of the 171 districts that had started desegregation. (This compares to 931 black students in twenty-four districts in 1964-65.)[180]

New Guidelines

Just as the state seemed to be meeting the requirements of the Civil Rights Act of 1964, word came that the "freedom of choice" plans were under review by the Office of Education. Reports indicated that, under "freedom of choice," desegregation was being left up to black children and their parents rather than to the school boards.[181] Commissioner Ford contacted Harold Howe II, U.S. commissioner of education, to express his concern about making changes in the federal guidelines. He said major changes to "speed up" desegregation would be "grossly unfair" to local school boards. He thought the present guidelines had not been in effect long enough for local school officials to implement their desegregation plans. Ford said, "My feeling is that it would be breaking faith with the school boards to make major revisions this year when the plans cover three years. We should operate another year and perhaps two more years under the present guidelines. Then they can change, when they live up to their moral commitments on the plans this year."

Ford said that the progress that year, as indicated by the nearly 6,300 black students being in desegregated schools, was deceiving. A few plans were approved as late as only two weeks before and numerous plans were not approved until after school began. Parents were naturally hesitant about transferring their children during the year. He predicted that if the same guidelines were in effect the next fall, desegregation would "be increased materially—perhaps by 200% or 300%."[182]

Dr. W. H. Townsend, president of the Council on Community Affairs (COCA) told Howe in a letter in January 1966 that the guidelines needed "considerable revision" because desegregation in Arkansas had been progressing at a "snail's pace." "It is the desire and prayer of the Negro leaders who constitute COCA that you will not be influenced by those who contend that after 12 years more time is needed," Townsend wrote to Howe. "Present guidelines have failed miserably as a method of change from a system of segregation to desegregation and we plead for guideline changes designed to accelerate desegregation."[183]

In March 1966, the Office of Education announced new guidelines that required any district receiving federal aid to end any discriminatory practices in faculty hiring and move toward ending separate systems for white and black students. The new plans were intended to ensure that the districts using "freedom of choice" plans were making progress in closing the small, inadequate schools for black or other minority students.[184]

Districts would have several alternatives for beginning faculty desegregation, and an integrated staff would not be required in every school within a district. U.S. Commissioner Howe explained, "Race, color or national origin may not be a factor in hiring, assigning, promoting or firing teachers and other professional staff. Staff desegregation for the 1966–67 school year must include progress in the desegregation of the regular teaching staff beyond what was accomplished in 1965–66 and there must be a significant start on this in those districts that have not yet begun faculty desegregation." He asked teachers' associations to help smooth the way.[185]

The new requirements on school faculty and staff provided that when one or more teacher or staff members were displaced as a result of desegregation "no staff vacancy in the school system [could] be filled through recruitment from outside the system unless the school officials [could] show that no such displaced staff member [was] qualified to fill the vacancy." Each school system also had to remove discrimination in transportation, athletics, and extracurricular activities.[186]

Howe said there would be more compliance reviews, field visits, and investigations by the Office of Education to determine whether the districts were indeed making quality education available to all students. In a district with a sizeable percentage of black or other minority students, Office of Education representatives would be guided by these criteria:

1) If a significant percentage of the students, such as 8-9%, transferred from segregated schools for the 1965-66 year, transfers of at least twice that percentage normally would be expected for the 1966-67 year.

2) If there was a smaller percentage, such as 4-5%, a substantial increase would be expected for next fall to make the total at least triple the 1965-66 percentage.

3) If no students transferred, then a very substantial start would be expected to enable the school system to catch up as quickly as possible.[187]

Commissioner Ford was disappointed that the Office of Education had changed the guidelines. He said in a September 1966 interview that he thought the new guidelines were politically inspired and the result of special interest groups rather than educators. He said that although he disagreed and opposed the new guidelines, it was his policy in life "to make the best of each situation as it arises and to live with those things that you cannot prevent."[188]

There were a couple of other exchanges between Howe and Ford after the new guidelines were announced. In April 1966, Ford declined Howe's invitation to come to Washington to hear further explanation of the new guidelines. Ford said he could not go to Washington anytime soon and that a representative from the Office of Education had explained the new guidelines recently at a meeting in Little Rock.[189]

A couple of months later, Howe sent out a memo warning state education departments that they had to enforce compliance with the new guidelines. The memo said that "failure by the state agencies to fulfill their obligations in enforcing compliance by school districts might jeopardize the continued participation of the entire state in federally assisted programs." Ford took issue with the memo. He said that enforcing the guidelines was specifically entrusted to federal agencies and that state agencies had no real enforcing power or obligation. "The obligation is to report noncompliance as you find it," he said. "Our commitment as I interpret it lies in being truthful with the United States office."[190]

HEW Sets Deadline for Completion of Desegregation

In November 1967, the U.S. Department of Health, Education and Welfare set a deadline for the completion of public school desegregation in the South. Districts were told that they had to complete the task of integration by the fall of 1969. Deadlines would vary by individual district because some districts had to complete construction, some had especially large numbers of students, and some had other complications that could cause a delay. This new approach had developed because "freedom of choice" plans were not working. When the plans did not work, districts had to develop new plans on their own, and the new plans had to be designed to eliminate dual systems completely.[191]

At the time of this announcement, Arkansas had eighty-six districts that were fully desegregated and 132 districts that were partially desegregated. There were still 171 all-white districts and six all-black districts in the state.[192] Ford said that one-fourth or fewer of Arkansas's biracial districts would be affected by the new directive. Ninety of the biracial districts had already integrated all grades. He was confident that Arkansas would make it through this new directive as well. He said, "We will win through on our desegregation problems. I'm not at all sure that two years is enough time but we are on the whole making significant progress and in many places satisfactory progress.

My guess is that the directive is politically timed to help bail out the Great Society."[193]

This attitude would continue as the Department of Education took another positive step in July 1968 when it named Earl Willis of Little Rock as a consultant to local school boards on desegregation. Willis had joined the Department of Education in 1965 and was known as a non-controversial educator who had the ability to work with both whites and blacks. Willis said that he would be available to work with any district that needed help.[194]

By the fall of 1969, about 53,000 of the approximately 100,000 black students in Arkansas were attending school in a desegregated district. About 40,000 of these students were in districts that had abolished the dual system in all grades. The others were in districts that had abolished the dual system only at certain grade levels, such as 1–6 or 7–12. An estimated 1,500 students were in nine districts that had forfeited federal aid in failing to comply with desegregation guidelines. Steps had been taken in ten others to withhold funds for non-compliance. These districts were declared ineligible for any new commitment of federal funds and eventually would lose the funds received under earlier commitments if they refused to desegregate. Appeals had been made and were pending for five of these districts.[195]

By November 1969, when the U.S. Supreme Court handed down a decision regarding desegregation in Mississippi, the state of Arkansas had 135 districts being run as unitary systems, having abolished the dual school system. About thirty more of the 215 biracial districts had plans that had already been approved. But still, only 49% of all black students in Arkansas were attending integrated schools. The Court's decision in Mississippi would result in lawsuits against non-complying districts by the spring of 1970.[196]

Threats of Lawsuits Bring Compliance

In April 1970, thirty-nine districts in Arkansas were informed that they faced lawsuits for failure to comply with the Civil Rights Act of 1964. Governor Winthrop Rockefeller asked the U.S. Justice Department for more time and was granted an extension. The new deadline was May 6, 1970. Three days after the deadline, Commissioner Ford informed the Justice Department that six districts in the state were refusing to comply. The other thirty-three remaining districts said they would try to comply voluntarily. They were working out an acceptable plan to achieve integration before the May 15 deadline the Justice Department had set.[197]

The Justice Department filed suit in federal court in July 1970 against nine Arkansas school districts: Cotton Plant, England, Hazen, Helena-West Helena, Holly Grove, Wabbaseka, Watson Chapel, Bradley, and Thornton. Federal judge Oren Harris issued an order requiring the districts to "seek to develop in conjunction with the Office of Education acceptable plans of operation that meet the requirements of desegregation decisions of the United States Supreme Court and U.S. Eighth Circuit Court of Appeals in St. Louis." The plans had to provide for the immediate conversion of the districts "to unitary, nondiscriminatory systems." Harris ordered the districts and the Justice Department to report by July 24 on whether they had been able to reach an agreement. If not, both sides would file their own plans by July 31. He would hold hearings during the week of August 10.[198]

Six of the nine districts reached an agreement before the lawsuits came to trial. The other three—Wabbaseka, Watson Chapel, and Hazen—were ordered to abolish their dual systems in the fall of 1970. Of the 215 biracial districts in the state, 137 had completed the transition to a unitary system by the end of the 1969–70 school year. The remaining seventy-eight biracial districts completed desegregation in the fall of 1970. The number of black students attending desegregated schools doubled. The Department of Education estimated that

113,000 black students were in desegregated schools in 1969–70, and well over 200,000 in the 1970–71 school year. Sixteen years after the *Brown* decision, Arkansas public schools finally finished integration.[199]

In 1972, the Arkansas Department of Education announced that it intended to take the lead in helping districts solve educational problems connected with integration. Commissioner Ford and Earl Willis, the department's desegregation consultant, said that the "legal phase of school desegregation" was completed with the establishment of unitary school systems but that the state needed to figure out "how might an educational program be developed that meets the needs of all students and attracts the support of both races?" They thought the department should assume leadership in helping districts handle the tensions and other problems in the schools and help the districts build an educational program that served both black and white children's needs.

To accomplish this, the department's professional staff attended sessions that would help them become more sensitive to the problems faced by blacks and whites in desegregated classrooms. The Arkansas Technical Assistance and Consultative Center (ATAC) at Ouachita Baptist University conducted the sessions. It was known for assisting school systems with desegregation problems. The department staff, particularly those who worked regularly in the schools, needed to acquire some expertise in talking with administrators and teachers about racial problems. Mr. Willis said, "There is need for recognition of those specific areas in which conflict inevitably develops and of how programs can be designed to prevent situations in which loss of face by one side or the other becomes necessary."

Dr. Ed Coulter of the ATAC staff said that black students had simply been assimilated into the formerly all-white systems, losing the traditions of their schools, such as the school song, colors, and mascot or team names. He said it would be helpful if whites thought about how they would feel if the reverse happened. He said something needed to be done to restore some social activities in many schools that had abandoned them. Many social activities had been discontinued because they would have to be integrated, which could cause trouble.[200]

The Department of Education also made efforts to improve job opportunities for minorities in education. In March 1974, the state Board of Education adopted an affirmative action plan that established numerical goals for minority hiring. It also established guidelines for reporting on the availability of qualified minorities and the grouping of job classifications.[201]

Chapter 7: The Birth of Vocational-Technical Schools

If ever there was anyone who had the requisite background, knowledge, and skills to establish a vocational-technical education system for Arkansas, it was Arch Ford. His service as an educational advisor in the Civilian Conservation Corps (CCC) for six years gave him a close-up, personal view of the need for vocational-technical education in Arkansas. He saw young men come through his CCC camp who just wanted to be able to make a decent living for their families during the hard times of the Depression. He saw what a bit of vocational and technical training could do to help them learn the skills of a trade so that they could return home and make a living.

That work experience took him to the state Department of Education as supervisor of vocational education, and it was his expertise in vocational education that paved his way to the commissioner job. The chairman of the state Board of Education said that the board liked the fact that he had competency in both vocational and general education.[202]

Creating a Statewide System of Vocational-Technical Schools

Arch Ford and others who saw the importance of vocational-technical education began to campaign for a system of vocational schools in the state in the mid-1950s to help create skilled workers as Arkansas became more industrialized. Work started in 1953, with a study being done on the need for vocational education in the state.[203]

In an article in *Arkansas Union Farmer* in 1957, Ford argued that area trade schools were needed in Arkansas to train men leaving their farms for the city. Their wives, sons, and daughters also needed training so that they could get jobs in the various industrial trades. He said, "About 15% of industrial workers must be highly skilled either through training received in a good trade school or training at the professional level. This is the group of employees which constitutes the bottleneck in securing new industry in a state like Arkansas. The majority of workers are semi-skilled or operators and can be trained in a few weeks....Arkansas is in need of a program for the training of skilled workers."[204]

The Arkansas General Assembly passed legislation in 1957 that created a Board of Vocational Education and gave it the authority to operate "regional schools for training in trades, occupations and arts and sciences." The legislation required that at least one school be established in each congressional district and that there not be more than ten in all the state. The schools would be required to meet federal standards required for accreditation of vocational and rehabilitation courses. Students would not have to pay until they finished the course. The Board of Vocational Education would make arrangements for the students to earn money to pay for part or all of their expenses.[205] In actuality, vocational-technical education in the state would be directed by the state Department of Education. There would be a Board of Vocational Education, but it would be made up of members from the state Board of Education.

The act also said that the board had to consider trends in industrial development in the state as well as the concentration of population and industry when selecting the sites. The General Assembly appropriated only $500,000, which was enough to build and equip only one vocational-technical school. The competition would be fierce among cities that wanted to be selected as the site for the school.[206]

Governor Orval Faubus appointed the Advisory Council on Vocational Education to work with the board on policy matters regarding the new school. The council was to be composed of one representative each from industry, business, agriculture, labor, and homemaking, as well as a member from the House of Representatives and a member from the Senate.

Applications were received from Arkadelphia, Batesville, Benton-Bauxite, Blytheville, Brinkley, Camden, Conway, De Queen, Fayetteville, Forrest City, Fort Smith, Hope, Hot Springs, Jacksonville, Little Rock, Magnolia, Malvern, Mena, Newport, Osceola, Paragould, Pine Bluff, Prescott, and Russellville. Virtually all of the cities offered free sites because the legislature had not appropriated enough to also buy the land. Delegations from each city made a presentation to the board explaining why they thought the new school should be located in their city.[207]

Many assumed that the first school would be located in Little Rock. John P. Bethell of Prairie County, who sponsored the legislation in 1957, said, "It was certainly the intention of the committee which did the preliminary work and of the legislature that the first school be located in Little Rock where it can serve the most people," Bethell said. "I want this first school to have every chance of being a success so that other schools can be established in the future."[208]

Bethell said he did not approve of the method used in picking three preferred sites. He submitted a resolution to the Arkansas Legislative Council saying that the action of the board was in violation of the intention of the General Assembly, and he ordered the board to select Little Rock. He said, "They ignored the requirement of the law to select a site which would serve the most people and took those which made the best bids." He said the Legislative Council needed to take action immediately because the board intended to visit the three sites they had selected on Monday and Tuesday and that a final decision might be made early in the next week.[209]

Commissioner Ford's response was that he would send the resolution to the board as soon as he got a copy. He said he did not think the council action would stop the visits to the three cities. Another council member, Representative Paul Van Dalsem, from

Perry County, warned the council members "not to faint" when they heard him support something for Pulaski County, but he felt that the school would serve more students if it were located in the central part of the state.[210]

Representative Marion Crank of Little River County, who had been part of the study that was done earlier, said he was not supporting Little Rock. He explained, however, that he also did not want the vocational school to be located in a city that had a state college: "We visited the vocational schools in Louisiana and we found the poorest schools and the worst attitudes in college towns. These vocational schools should be located in a place where they will be the most important institution, not a secondary one."[211]

Bethell and Van Dalsem went to see Governor Faubus the next week to protest what they termed a "cut and dried deal" to put the institution at Magnolia. Faubus said he was not going to interfere with the Board of Education's decision on a site for the vocational school. He said he had not intended to express a personal preference, but he said he believed that the opinion of the sponsors from the legislature should carry weight with the board in its decision.[212]

The board ignored the Legislative Council resolution and went on with its plans to inspect the sites at Pine Bluff, Magnolia, and Camden. Pine Bluff had offered a ten-acre site adjacent to the municipal airport, Grider Field. Magnolia had offered four sites: one in the city's industrial area and two blocks from Southern State College; another in Smith Field, an athletic area that Southern State's trustees offered to lease; a third in the Columbia County Development Corporation; and a 75-acre tract on U.S. Highway 82. Camden had offered a site within the Shumaker Naval Ammunition Depot as well as two other sites with ten acres each. All had been offered at no cost to the state.[213]

In an interview that week, Bethell said, "That resolution seems to be ignored so now we will go into court and stop the whole thing until the 1959 legislature meets. Then we will repeal the act and take the whole matter away from the Board of Education. It should never have been given to them in the first place." He said he had been planning a vocational setup in Arkansas "for five years and I am not going to let it be ruined by the Arkansas Education Association, the Board of Education or anyone else." He said that the "very purpose of putting this school in Little Rock was to take advantage of all of the various industrial operations for coordination with the training of these young people." Bethell said he had "nothing against Magnolia. It's a fine city but we don't want this vocational school down on the Louisiana state line."[214]

Despite all this, Pine Bluff would subsequently be selected as the site of first vocational-technical school. Ground was broken in early May 1958, and work was completed on the construction of the Arkansas Vocational-Technical School in February 1959. Leon Coker, superintendent of Des Arc School District, was selected as the head of the school, which opened that fall.

The curriculum was determined by a special thirty-man committee. The length of the courses ranged from nine months to two years. Classes would meet six days a week. Night classes would be three hours on three nights a week. There were also part-time courses. The school was in session year round. Courses offered were welding, sheet metal work, machine shop, auto mechanics, auto body, woodworking, electronics, radio and television repair, drafting, commercial cooking and baking, and practical nursing. Extension courses took care of other types of technical training that might be needed in the state.[215]

When the school opened on September 21, 1959, there were 224 enrollees[216] for the fall semester. By spring, there were 509 adults attending the school.[217] Most of the students who completed the programs stayed in the state. The jobs they secured were usually in small industries in the state, although these students were in high demand in any large industry because of their basic knowledge of machinery.[218]

Commissioner Ford continued to advocate for vocational-technical education. He told the Board of Education in a meeting in September 1961 that the state needed to step up its vocational training program to offset the unemployment caused by automation, as automation was creating a demand for training and retraining of workers. Arkansas would be increasingly affected in the future by this trend. He thought that the main obstacle was money. He said, "We have enough federal money available to maintain several trade schools in the state but the state could not afford to pay for their operation now on the same basis as the one in Pine Bluff. The Pine Bluff school operates on a budget of $215,000 which includes about $45,000 in matching federal aid."[219]

The Board of Education had already proposed the building of another vocational-technical school, but the legislature rejected a $275,000 appropriation for it in the previous special session. Just as the Arkansas Vocational-Technical School was getting ready to celebrate its second birthday, the board was able to get legislative approval for a second school.[220]

Petit Jean Vocational-Technical School

Morrilton, Magnolia, and Fort Smith were the main contenders in the competition for the next vocational-technical school. Morrilton business and political leaders teamed up to present a well-documented and persuasive bid. Lieutenant Governor Nathan Gordon led the Morrilton group, which included Conway County judge Tom Scott, Conway County sheriff Marlin Hawkins, and state Representative Loid Sadler. They were the only delegation to appear in person before the Board of Education and the Advisory Council for Vocational Education. Senator Knox Nelson of Pine Bluff served as council chair, and Representative G. D. Smith Jr. of Lincoln County served

Petit Jean Vocational-Technical School when it opened in 1963. *Photo courtesy of the University of Arkansas Community College at Morrilton*

as vice-chairman.[221]

Lt. Governor Gordon said that Morrilton was in a well-populated and progressive area with a good road network, strong educational facilities, and the support of an eleven-county area. The school would also fit into the development of the Arkansas River Valley, he said. Furthermore, the community had banded together to offer, without cost, sites of twenty to thirty acres. Some of the tracts bordered a proposed interchange on Interstate 40 regarded by several council members as extremely valuable land.

Morrilton was selected as the site of the new school. Governor Faubus expressed complete satisfaction with the selection of Morrilton instead of Fort Smith, saying that he believed that the Morrilton site would be a better location for the training of rural residents in skilled industries and trades.[222] An *Arkansas Gazette* writer reporting on the selection said, "From all indications, the school at Morrilton will be a big success. The community and area interest is there as is the population from which the students will come." But he also said "it was regarded as a generally open secret in the legislature last year that Morrilton had the inside track." The presence in the State Capitol of Marlin Hawkins as a one-man lobby supported the rumor. Since the passage of the school act, a couple of legislators indicated that they voted with the assumption that Morrilton was to be the site.[223]

At its March 1962 board meeting, the Board of Education selected Thurston Kirk to be the director of the new Petit Jean Vocational-Technical School. Kirk, a veteran of World War II, had been a $7,000-a-year counselor at the Arkansas Vocational-Technical School in Pine Bluff. He assumed his new duties as director on July 1, 1962, to work with the architect and provide advice in the development of the curriculum for the new school. His salary was not announced, but the director of the Pine Bluff school made $8,200 a year. Edward Gordon of Morrilton, Perron Jones of Searcy, and T. C. Cogbill Jr. of Star City were also named to work with the state Advisory Council on developing the curriculum. Ford said that the professional staff of the Department of Education would work with the council and with Morrilton interests in developing a course of study best suited for the area. The board would have the final say on what was taught there.[224]

Construction of Petit Jean Vocational-Technical School began in early 1963. At the March 1963 Board of Education meeting, the board announced that the school would be completed about July 1 and would open in September. It also authorized the installation of air conditioning in most of the facilities; only the shops were to be without air conditioning. This commitment to spend an additional $20,000 for air conditioning was very unusual at this time.[225]

The dedication ceremony was held August 25, 1963. Governor Faubus, Lieutenant Governor Nathan Gordon, Chairman of the Board of Education Marvin Bird, Commissioner Arch Ford, and several other state officials attended the ceremony. Members of the Governor's Advisory Council and the state Board of Education also attended.

Conway County sheriff Marlin Hawkins introduced Governor Faubus, who gave the dedicatory address. Faubus told the almost 4,000 people at the dedication that vocational training was necessary because they had entered an age of specialization. He said more

Dedication ceremony at Petit Jean Vocational-Technical School, August 25, 1963. Left to right: Thurston Kirk, director of Petit Jean Vocational-Technical School; Commissioner Arch Ford; Perron Jones, member of the State Board of Education; Governor Orval Faubus; Jack Rupert, head of the State Vocational-Technical Department; and Rev. Earl Smith. *Photo courtesy of the University of Arkansas Community College at Morrilton*

schools would be built in the state but emphasized that they would be purposeless without students. The Morrilton Chamber of Commerce had a chicken dinner for dignitaries attending the dedication ceremony.[226]

The school cost $240,000 to build. The director, Thurston Kirk, said that although the school would mainly serve an eleven-county area, it would be open to any Arkansas resident in the state age sixteen or older. He also said that eighteen of the twenty-three staff members were recruited from industrial firms.

Courses offered at the school would be appliance service, auto mechanics, landscaping and horticulture, machine shop, office practices (including typing, shorthand, and bookkeeping), practical nursing, printing, welding, diesel mechanics, heavy equipment operation and maintenance, drafting and surveying, building construction, and data processing. The school opened on September 16, 1963.[227] In 1965, the board approved an expansion to the facility to add an auditorium and a shop building for welding and diesel training.[228]

Planning for More Trade Schools

In September 1963, Orval Faubus appointed an advisory council to work with the Board of Education on a plan to expand the vocational-technical school program. The council would help in locating new schools and working out the financing of the operations. Money for the first two schools had come out of the Public School Fund, but everyone involved realized that there needed to be a better source of funding. Governor Faubus said that a special fund supported by a tax should be set up within the Revenue Stabilization Act.[229]

Commissioner Ford predicted that the development of the vocational-technical school program would accelerate, because of the popularity of the existing two schools. He believed the next school would be built within the next two years as soon as the money from surplus revenues became available. He anticipated that the other schools would be built even more quickly because the public was demanding them.

He realized that financing the schools was a big issue. He said that a permanent revenue source outside the public school fund had to be found, both for construction and operation. He also added, "Drawing on surpluses to finance construction is not the way." He warned that letting the trade school program get involved in politics would be dangerous. He thought the decision should be left to the board, advisory committee, and professional school staff.[230]

The 1963 legislature allocated $550,000 for the construction of a third vocational-technical school if money was available from surplus funds. Again, several cities vied to get the new school. Blytheville and Osceola teamed up to offer a site to serve both. Pocahontas offered an elementary school building and its grounds. Magnolia resubmitted. Marion, Boone, Newton, Baxter, Searcy, and Stone Counties united to explore the possibility of starting a trade school to serve all six counties. Many educators and business leaders were coming to believe that such a school could reverse the school dropout trend and provide needed manpower for industries.[231]

It would be 1965 before funding was available to build another vocational-technical school. In June 1965, the Board of Education announced plans for eight new schools. Ford said that enough money was available to start construction on the first four and the others would be built as money became available. By July 1, 1965, $750,000 in state funds had been matched with federal funds to start construction.

Because of the restrictions that had been placed on site selection by the 1957 legislature, the next schools would have to be placed in the other four congressional districts. The sites would be selected by ballot by the Board of Education, and twenty-six towns and areas were listed on the ballot. Those chosen were Blytheville-Osceola, Searcy, Ozark, and Hope. The other sites chosen for when money became available were El Dorado, Marked Tree, Forrest City, and Harrison.[232]

In July 1965, the Vocational Education Committee of the state Board of Education released the names that had been chosen for the eight new vocational-technical schools. They also named directors for the first four and gave a partial list of the courses that would be offered at each school.

• Blytheville-Osceola—**Cotton Boll Vocational-Technical School**; Charles Ross, an area vocational education supervisor; auto mechanics, machine shop, office practice, sheet metal and drafting.

• Searcy—**Foothills Vocational-Technical School**; Luther Hardin, a vocational agriculture teacher in Searcy Public Schools; cosmetology, farm equipment mechanics, machine shop, office practice, practical nursing, electric motor repair and body repair.

• Ozark—**Arkansas Valley Vocational-Technical School**; Alvin Vest, superintendent of County Line School District in Franklin County; food processing technology, cosmetology, barbering, office practice, radio-television service, and auto mechanics.

• Hope—**Red River Vocational-Technical School**; J. W. Rose, a member of the Arkansas Vocational Technical School faculty at Pine Bluff.

• Marked Tree—**Delta Vocational-Technical School**; agricultural technology, farm equipment mechanics, welding, practical nursing, and office practice.

• Forrest City—**Crowley's Ridge Vocational-Technical School**; electronics, practical nursing, machine shop, auto mechanics, drafting, and office practice.

• Harrison—**Twin Lakes Vocational-Technical School**; appliance service, machine shop, practical nursing, auto mechanics, office practice, radio-television service, and cooking.

• El Dorado—**Oil Belt Vocational-Technical School**; chemical technology, instrumentation and electronics, auto mechanics, mechanical drafting, machine shop and equipment maintenance, practical nursing, and office practice.[233]

By 1966, the legislature had allocated $1.5 million for the construction of the other four vocational-technical schools, at Harrison, Forrest City, Marked Tree, and El Dorado. At its March 1966 meeting, the Board of Education announced that bids would be opened on May 17.[234] Because of the addition of the other schools in the state, the board also had to rename the Arkansas Vocational-Technical School in Pine Bluff. It became Pines Vocational-Technical School.[235]

The Board of Education gave final approval to the courses at six trade schools at its May 1966 meeting. It also approved courses for Fort Smith Community College, which became a public facility and for Arkansas Agricultural, Mechanical, and Normal School at Pine Bluff, which would begin offering vocational courses. Cotton Boll Vocational-Technical School at Burdette was also listed as a new trade school.[236]

That summer, it was announced that a new technical school would be established at Camden and would offer such courses as industrial chemistry, electronics, drafting, aviation, and hydraulics. It would be located in the buildings on the old Shumaker Naval Ammunition Depot. David H. Pryor, who was running for the Fourth District congressional seat that year, said that the establishment of a technical school near Camden would increase substantially the number of skilled workers and technicians in southern Arkansas and thereby encourage industries to locate in the area. "It is a known fact that one of the major reasons for failing to entice major industrial firms to move to South Arkansas has been the scarcity of skilled labor. Naturally companies want to locate in an area where they know they can find an abundance of highly trained people instead of having to move them there." Another advantage would be to keep the young people at home. He said, "Now we can train them in our own backyard and hopefully will be able to offer them the necessary incentive to stay here where they will be able to help contribute to the realization of the vast industrial potential of south Arkansas."[237]

Vocational Education in Secondary Schools

By 1970, there were eleven vocational-technical post-secondary schools in the state, and all of them were operating at near or full capacity. The Arkansas Advisory Council on Vocational Education recommended in April 1970 that vocational-technical education be shifted to high schools rather than expanding the post-secondary system that the state was operating. The board disagreed with the recommendations and approved a new plan in June to continue its program of building post-secondary vocational technical schools so that eventually there would be a vocational-technical school within driving distance of every student in the state who wanted to attend.

The board instead said that some supplementary vocational-technical courses would be added to about 200 high schools and that the state Department of Education would seek in the 1971–72 biennium to start "comprehensive" vocational programs in larger school districts. But the biggest reason for continuing with the existing post-secondary program was that funds for vocational high schools were not available.[238]

The next year, the Board of Education approved $100,000 grants to both the Conway and Russellville school districts to help build area vocational high schools. The state was already supporting two vocational high schools, in Little Rock and Fayetteville, and it would provide partial support for the two new schools once they were built. The legislature also provided aid for a vocational high school at Texarkana.[239]

Commissioner Ford gave the address at the dedication of the Conway Area Career Center in 1973, with approximately 5,300 people in attendance.[240] The center would serve students from the multiple districts in Faulkner County, providing classes in auto body, auto mechanics, machine shop, refrigeration, health occupations, radio and TV repair, construction, drafting, welding, home economics, accounting, and horticulture. It would also provide work-study opportunities for students.

Mobile Training Units

In 1968, Congress passed the Vocational Education Act, which was designed to provide exploratory vocational experiences in industrial machine trades. A mobile machine shop training unit, sponsored by the state Department of Education's Division of Vocational, Technical and Adult Education, would be used by selected or participating schools as a self-contained classroom and work area. The unit was a custom mobile trailer that was outfitted with ten lathe-mills, ten tool packages, ten vertical milling machines, and twenty sets of instructional materials. It had twenty adjustable desks that could serve as drafting tables, twenty student chairs, a chalkboard, a teacher desk, a projector, and storage. There would be three classes during the day and one class at night. Sixty hours of instruction would be provided for each class at each location.[241]

In the fall of 1972, four small school districts in western Arkansas—with a combined secondary enrollment of 1,032—joined together to offer "round robin" mobile educational facilities. Mobile classroom units for machine shop, construction, and refrigeration and air conditioning, as well as electricity and electronics, would be rotated among the four districts. Of the four districts, only two had previously offered vocational courses of any kind.[242]

Vocational Training for Inmates

In 1970, the Board of Education voted to spend federal funds to help the state Board of Corrections start a vocational education program for inmates at the state penitentiary. Commissioner Arch Ford said that the board had approved the $200,000 expenditure because it thought vocational training for inmates had "high priority in the minds of both the governor and the legislature." He said the Department of Education would start to work immediately to help establish the program.

Commissioner of Corrections Robert Sarver said that the Department of Corrections had received an appropriation of $144,000 from the legislature to renovate the facilities for such a program and that the Department of Education funds would provide the revenue for starting the training. He said that one of the reforms most needed at the prison was a program to train inmates so that they could obtain a job when they were released. Most of the training would be done at the Tucker unit, where young offenders were held.[243]

The Rise of Community Colleges

In 1972, the state Advisory Commission on Community Junior Colleges proposed that when any junior college district was formed, it should be merged with any vocational school in that area and placed under the control of the junior college. This essentially meant that the vocational school would then be controlled by the Department of Higher Education, which supervised junior colleges and four-year colleges.

Two-year colleges had started as a grassroots movement in the mid-1960s in Arkansas. The movement was part of a national trend to provide students with an extension of high school that would, for some, end in a terminal degree but, for others, would prepare them to move on to a four-year college. At that time, Commissioner Ford spoke out in support of such a school. He even liked the idea that they would be called community colleges rather than junior colleges. But a decade later, this proposal for merging community colleges and vocational schools was vehemently opposed by the state Board of Education and the Department of Education.[244]

The vocational-technical staff of the Department of Education drafted a five-page memorandum to the Board of Education opposing the recommendation. The vocational-technical committee of the board met with the Advisory Commission to discuss the problems they thought might arise from such a merger. Four arguments were given against the merger. The first was the concern that a junior-college administrator would be inclined to restrict vocational education and favor academic programs if faced with a limited budget. Vocational programs required more money for equipment and therefore would be more expensive to run than academic programs. Academic programs had to follow strict guidelines in order for the students to meet the requirements to transfer to a four-year college. The second argument given was that some young people would not want to go to a merged institution because it would be more of an academic atmosphere. Instead, they wanted technical skills. A third argument was that instructors with occupational experience could be undervalued in a system that placed academic qualifications on its instructors. A final argument was that there would not be much cost savings by combining the junior colleges and vocational-technical schools because they would be able to share very few facilities.

A 1967 law had authorized agreements between junior colleges and vocational-technical schools for the sharing of staff, facilities, and services. The department memo said that this arrangement should be tried before mergers. It proposed several steps for implementing that law, including permitting students to spend half of each day in each school if they wanted both kinds of subjects, allowing junior colleges to grant credit for courses taken at nearby vocational-technical schools and prorating the cost of operating any common facilities.[245] The merger did not happen at that time, but there was a strong sentiment among some educators that the state should be focusing on building more community colleges instead of vocational-technical schools. A similar proposal would emerge in 1991.

In a speech to the Conway Rotary Club in November 1967, Arch Ford gave strong support to both community colleges and vocational-technical schools. Although Arkansas had only two junior colleges at that time, Ford predicted that there could be as many as seven or eight opened in the next five years. He also predicted that "this junior college program eventually will find its way into central Arkansas but certainly not in Conway." He believed that the junior colleges "did not detract—they strengthen the senior institutions."[246]

Completing the Vocational-Technical System

Other vocational-technical schools would be completed in the years before Commissioner Ford retired. There were twenty-three schools in operation by the time he retired at the end of 1978. Little Rock finally got its school in early 1976 when Pulaski Vocational-Technical School was opened. In 1969, the state assumed operation of a facility that had been run by the Little Rock School District at the old East Side Junior High School since 1964. The legislature appropriated $972,000 to build and equip a new facility that was added to the $75,000 the school already had, making the total outlay nearly $1,050,000.

The new facility would be located on a 137-acre tract that once was part of the North Little Rock Veterans Administration Hospital. The 36,000-square-foot building, all on one level, was handicapped accessible. The school could double its course offerings to include business and office education, data processing, practical nursing, dental assistant training, welding, machine shop, all types of drafting, industrial equipment, metals testing, and applied mathematics and physics. The new building would accommodate 350 students.[247]

Act 1244 of 1991

Act 1244 of the 78th General Assembly would re-designate and redefine the mission of the post-secondary vocational-technical schools in 1991. The eleven existing schools throughout the state would be converted to two-year colleges. State authority for the schools was transferred from the Arkansas Board of Education to the Arkansas Board of Higher Education. Pines Vocational-Technical School became Southeast Arkansas Technical College in 1996 and then was renamed Southeast Arkansas College in 1998. Petit Jean Vocational-Technical School became Petit Jean Technical College in 1991 and was renamed Petit Jean College in 1997. Petit Jean College later joined the University of Arkansas system and became the University of Arkansas Community College at Morrilton.

Vocational-technical education for the adults of Arkansas was very important to Arch Ford, and he worked diligently to make sure that every person in the state could easily commute to a school for training. In a 1979 interview, he was asked what he wanted to be remembered for accomplishing during his tenure as commissioner of education. The first thing he mentioned was the statewide system of vocational-technical schools.[248]

Chapter 8: The Communist Threat and Economic Education

Desegregation was not the only national event that affected the development of Arkansas education. In the 1950s, a movement called McCarthyism swept the country. Joseph McCarthy, U.S. senator from Wisconsin, exploited the fear of communism to build his political career. His method was to accuse people of being communists, often without much evidence, and thereby ruin their careers. He was successful in his witch-hunt tactics until he accused the U.S. Army of being infested with communists. In the U.S. Army-McCarthy hearings, which were televised, Joseph McCarthy's true character was on display for all of America to see. He was censured by the U.S. Congress for "conduct unbecoming a member" and was voted out of office by his constituents. He died a few years later from problems associated with alcoholism.

The fear that communism could somehow find its way into Arkansas's public schools concerned many at that time. The state Department of Education was asked in September 1953 if it was possible for subversive information to be in Arkansas's public school textbooks. Commissioner Arch Ford made assurences that with the system in place for textbook selection, it would be highly unlikely that communist ideas could slip through. He and his staff believed it was extremely unlikely that communists could get their propaganda into school books in the state even if they concentrated all of their efforts in this direction.

Commissioner Ford went on to explain how the textbook selection process worked. As commissioner, he appointed a five-member examination team for every textbook that was offered by publishers. The examination team read the books, consulted with classroom teachers, and made recommendations to the Board of Education about which books should be adopted. While he assured the board, he also cautioned, "I'm in general sympathy with a policy of alertness but I'm against book burning."[249]

In November 1953, the Department of Education was asked by the Arkansas Legislative Council to submit for its study fifteen sociology textbooks currently being used in Arkansas high schools or colleges that had been listed as "leftist" by a Dr. A. W. Hobbs. George Benson, president of Harding College, had recently mentioned the sociology texts in an article he had written for the college newsletter, and Representative James R. Campbell of Garland County had taken note of it.[250]

The fear of communism in the state was seen in other areas as well. In 1954, incumbent governor Francis Cherry used a McCarthy-like tactic against his opponent Orval Faubus when he realized Faubus might actually beat him in a run-off election. When he was younger, Faubus had attended Commonwealth College in Mena, a college formed by left-wing activists and socialists who were later found to be connected to the Communist Party of the United States. Faubus claimed he had spent only a few weeks there, but it later came out that he had attended college there for a year and was even elected student body president. The Cherry campaign to paint Faubus as a communist backfired, however, because many Arkansans were getting weary of the "witch-hunt" tactics of McCarthyism by 1954. Faubus defeated Cherry for the Democratic nomination and went on to win the general election.

Even so, the threat of communism still lingered over the Faubus administration for the first few terms he was in office. In 1956, the Arkansas General Assembly was becoming increasingly reactionary. For example, it tried to pass a bill that would require state employees and teachers to sign a loyalty oath and swear they belonged to no subversive organizations. Those who refused would be fired. For his part, Faubus said it was not possible to obtain loyalty that way and refused to support it. In 1958, the legislature passed a new version of the law as part of its attack on integration. It required all state employees and teachers to list all the organizations they belonged to or supported financially. For political reasons, Faubus signed it this time. The law received only cursory attention at the time, but when teachers at the public schools and state colleges were asked to swear their allegiance to the state and nation and list their organizations, many rebelled. In 1960, on a vote of five to four, the Arkansas Supreme Court declared that the law was unconstitutional. It caused a lot of resentment that lingered for years.[251]

Faubus blamed the communists for the civil rights movement in the 1960s. He even signed a bill that made membership in the Communist Party a felony punishable by six years in prison. Faubus also ranted against the *Arkansas Gazette*, claiming it had communist sympathies because of its stand on integration. "The *Gazette* seldom endorses any cause or action unless it is atheistic, immoral, or pro-Communist," he wrote in 1966.[252]

The state Department of Education was ordered by a legislative directive to root out subversive and "un-American" philosophies from the public textbook program. None were found, but Commissioner Ford suggested that certain key legislators might want to sit alongside some local school personnel and take a closer look.[253]

With this heightened sensitivity to communist threats in Arkansas, there was a lot of pressure put on the schools to "root out" communists or any kind of communist influence. There were even calls for courses in anti-communism to be taught to every student in the public schools. Commissioner Ford decided that the Department of Education should develop a plan for dealing with this paranoia in a positive way. It was this perceived communist threat that led to the development of two major advancements in Arkansas education:

economic education and educational television. The development of educational television will be addressed in the next chapter.

The Arkansas Council on Economic Education (ACEE)

Joe Ford, Arch Ford's son, graduated from Conway High School in 1955. He attended Arkansas State College, then transferred to the University of Arkansas in Fayetteville. He said he remembered coming home in the fall of 1956 and telling his father about an economics class he was taking that semester. He had enjoyed learning about how the country's economic system operates, and he realized how important it was to understand that. He remembered asking his father why there could not be a class like that at the high school level. He wondered why students had to wait until they were in college to take an economics course. He recalled that his father did not say much then on the matter, but, later, the Arkansas Council on Economic Education was formed.[254]

Coupled with this, in the spring of 1961, Arch Ford outlined a positive three-point program he thought should be undertaken in Arkansas to promote capitalism and combat communism:

• Develop a program called Strengthen America, which would stress appreciation of our country with patriotic overtones for elementary grades.

• Develop a study of communism and other "isms" at the high school level.

• Develop a program of economic education for all grades.

It was Commissioner Ford's philosophy that the United States' own economic system produced the highest standard of living in the world, and learning about this system was necessary in a society in which decisions are made by the people.[255] He also thought that high school students needed to understand the American economic system if they were to fully understand how economic communism was a threat to capitalism.

That summer, Arch Ford named Bessie Moore, supervisor for elementary education at the state Department of Education, to lead a new initiative for economic education. Under the leadership of Arch Ford and Bessie Moore, Arkansas would become a nationally recognized model in economic education. They are considered the "father" and "mother" of economic education in Arkansas.

While Bessie Moore was working on her master's degree at the University of Connecticut, she had learned about an organization in New York City called the Joint Council on Economic Education. Dr. Philmore Wass, executive director for the Connecticut Council on Economic Education, was on the committee for her master's work. When he heard about her new responsibility, he suggested that she go to New York to visit the executive director of the Joint Council on Economic Education. He also suggested that she extend her stay at the university so she could attend an economic education workshop that was being conducted there. She stayed for the workshop and made plans to go to New York.[256]

In the fall of 1961, the Arkansas Legislative Council set up a committee to study the need for a law requiring a course about communism in all the schools. At a hearing about the matter, Commissioner Ford presented his three-point program for promoting capitalism and combating communism. The council decided that no special legislation was needed and complimented Ford and the department for their positive approach to the situation.

Bessie Moore stopped by the Joint Council on Economic Education that summer on her way to participate in a Crusade for Freedom tour of a Radio-Free-Europe facility in West Germany and Portugal. She visited with Dr. M. L. Frankel, the director of the Joint Council, and Dr. George Fersh, the assistant director. When she returned to Arkansas in October, she got to work on developing the economic program.

Commissioner Ford invited the Joint Council to send a representative to Arkansas to talk to two groups who met separately. The first group was made up of educators, while the second group was composed of business leaders from all facets of the economy. All agreed to support the creation of the Arkansas Council on Economic Education. This council would serve as an advisory group to the Department of Education, so it was decided that appointment to the council should be based upon the invitation of Ford. Those serving on the council would be selected based on four criteria: 1) the individual must be an outstanding citizen with an abiding interest in education, 2) the individual must recognize the need for economic education, 3) the individual must be respected by his or her peer group, and 4) the individual must be willing to adhere to the principles of objectivity and academic freedom.[257]

The Arkansas Council on Economic Education held its organizational meeting on February 27, 1962. More than fifty representatives from education, business, labor, and agriculture were invited. Dr. George Fersh from the Joint Council was on hand as a consultant. The council would be financed from private funds except for the salary and expenses of the director and some office expenses. It was decided that there should be an elected president from education who would focus on the economic education programs, while a chairman of the board would focus on the fundraising aspects of the organization. Bessie Moore was named the first executive director of the council. She served as director until her retirement in 1974.

Arch Ford said that the formation of the council would be an important step in Arkansas education. He said that the understanding of the American economy "developed in most high schools today is inadequate for effective citizenship." He said the main need was to teach students how to think objectively about economic issues.[258]

The council recognized that its first responsibility should be to provide in-service training for teachers in economics. It was too late for arrangements to be made for a summer workshop in Arkansas. By late May, however, the coordinator—working with help from the Joint Council—had arranged for acceptance of Arkansas teachers in nine widely scattered universities, from Brigham Young University in Utah to the University of Vermont. Teams of teachers from eleven school districts were chosen to attend those summer workshops.[259]

Moore also had to increase awareness of the need for economic education. An economic education breakfast was held at the annual meeting of the Arkansas Education Association. This breakfast would become an annual event. College teachers of economics and business devoted their annual meeting to economic education. A five-state meeting of elementary principals in Little Rock featured the importance of economic education. The Arkansas Association for Supervision and Curriculum Development devoted four sessions to economic education at its annual meeting.[260]

Another great opportunity came when Ouachita Baptist College in Arkadelphia got a grant to be used in a program of American studies. The college paid for all of the expenses of an economic education conference for teachers, school administrators, and laymen. Some 200 people learned about economic education at that conference.

"The American Economy"

In 1963, Arkansas was chosen by the Joint Council on Economic Education to be the pilot state for a three-year pilot project, along with the thirteen states that were members of the Southern States Work Conference. Arkansas had been chosen because it demonstrated and "accepted a sound understanding of the economic education program, was supported by the State Department through assignment of personnel, and involved productively leaders of education and the economy." A $41,000 budget was approved for the Arkansas Council to start making things happen.

Delegates were sent to the Southern States Work Conference to share the Arkansas program with the other states. Scholarships were awarded for Arkansans to attend other workshops and conferences. The council hired economic and education consultants and held conferences for college teachers. It also made preparations for use of the new CBS television network college course, "The American Economy," to be presented in the 1963–64 school year. The council distributed a curriculum guide for the program that had been produced by the Joint Council on Economic Education.[261]

Moore was also able to get more exposure for economic education through newsletters, brochures, and public service announcements. For instance, a one-minute advertisement about the Arkansas Council on Economic Education was shown before every session of the CBS economics course for teachers. It ran at 6:45 each morning, Monday through Friday, from September 24, 1963, to May 24, 1964. This course was endorsed by Commissioner Ford in a letter to all school administrators. Three colleges set up programs to offer college credit for the course.[262]

First ACEE Economic Education Workshops

The Arkansas Council on Economic Education conducted its first state economic education workshops in the summer of 1963. The first of the three sessions held that summer was at Ouachita Baptist College. Dr. Samuel P. McCutchen, head of the social studies department at New York University, conducted the week-long session, aided by Dr. James Calderwood, economist and professor in the School of Business Administration at the University of Southern California. The Ouachita session was limited to eighty Arkansas teachers of American history, and one hour of college credit was offered to participants. The courses included trips to observe industry, agriculture, banks, and power facilities.

The other two workshops were held concurrently at the University of Arkansas for Medical Sciences (UAMS) campus. One workshop was on conservation education, while the other was on economic education. Dr. George Fersh, the assistant director of the Joint Council on Economic Education, was the director of the workshops and was assisted in teaching the economics portion of the workshop by Professor Calvin Gall, University of Connecticut; Meno Lovenstein, Ohio State University; and Dr. Theral Herrick, executive director of the Michigan Council on Economic Education. The session was limited to 100 teachers who were offered three hours of college credit.[263]

Speakers at the workshop were Henry Ford II; Secretary of the Interior Stewart L. Udall; David Bell, administrator for the Agency for International Development in Washington DC and former director of the Budget Bureau; Seymour Brandwein from the Office of Manpower Development and Training in the Labor Department in Washington DC; Harry A. Shuford, president of the St. Louis Federal Reserve Bank; U.S. Representative Wilbur Mills of Kensett, Arkansas, who was chair of the House Ways and Means Committee; U.S. Senator John L. McClellan; Winthrop Rockefeller; Governor Faubus; and the vice president of the AFL-CIO, who represented George Meany, president of AFL-CIO.[264]

Arkansas Council on Economic Education newsletter highlighting the workshop held at UAMS June 23–July 12, 1963. Arch Ford is pictured with the workshop's featured speaker, Henry Ford II, who was chairman of the board of the Ford Motor Company. *Photo courtesy of Economics Arkansas*

The program touched on all aspects of the state's economy as well as the principles and performance of the American economic system. Those attending the workshop also learned about the institutions and organizations that participate in

David Rockefeller, president of Chase Manhattan Bank, New York City; Winthrop Rockefeller; Dr. George L. Fersh, associate director of the Joint Council on Economic Education; Arch Ford; and Council President Cass S. Hough at the 1963 economic education workshop. *Photo courtesy of Economics Arkansas*

the American economic system. In addition, they studied the economic policies and issues that were affecting the state and nation.[265]

The Arkansas economics program was now considered a "pilot" for the South and other parts of the nation. When he announced the workshop in March, Commissioner Ford said that there would be representatives from ten southern states and from Montana at the workshop.[266] The Sears, Roebuck Foundation donated $10,000 to the Arkansas Council on Economic Education, which paid for the expenses of the educators from these other states. The rest of the donation, which was presented to Bessie Moore by W. Clyde Greenway, who was vice president of the foundation, was used to award teachers and school administrators in Arkansas who made outstanding contributions to economic education.[267]

The workshop at UAMS was a resounding success. One of the most successful and productive innovations of the workshops had been the field trips. Groups were sent out to different sites and then came back the following day to share what they had learned with the whole group. Groups visited manufacturers, retailers, public utilities, newspapers, farms, and government enterprises.

Governor Faubus was also complimentary of the workshop. He said, "In my opinion, the high caliber of leaders appearing on the Economic Workshop program made it one of the most outstanding educational events to be presented in Arkansas. The fact that there was no bias to the agenda is evidence of the sincere desire to educate

David Mullins, president of the University of Arkansas; Rep. Wilbur Mills; Henry Ford II; and Arch Ford at the 1963 economic education workshop. *Photo courtesy of Economics Arkansas*

our teachers to the alternatives of a free society." [268]

Commissioner Ford spoke at the final meeting of the workshop. He declared that the Department of Education was committed to a program of economic education in the public schools. He said, "Outside of communication—the English language—economics is the most important area in our program. So let's put it there." He said the department had taken the steps toward "putting it there" by organizing the council, assigning personnel to the program, and co-sponsoring the workshop. In the future, he said, it should sponsor more such training sessions, help in the development of classroom materials at the state and local level, and promote a factual, objective presentation of the subject. He stated further that economics was a crucial subject that had to be taught in the schools. He argued that, though we are immersed in it in daily life, we are not born with knowledge of it, any more than we are born with a sense of racial intolerance. Economics had to be taught early in the school program because a large percentage of students would not finish high school. [269]

One of the requirements of the summer workshops was that the teachers had to attend a planning and sharing meeting in September. The teachers, accompanied by their superintendents, gathered to share enthusiasm, ideas, lessons, and plans for the year. This was a significant achievement because the meeting was scheduled on what Bessie Moore called "a football Saturday." [270] This would be a regular feature in the years to come.

Other Notable Economic Education Highlights

At its November 1963 meeting, the state Board of Education made a recommendation to the Advisory Council on Teacher Education and Certification for the Arkansas Department of Education. It recommended that three semester hours of economics be required for certification of elementary school teachers. This recommendation led to the greater involvement of Arkansas colleges in economic education and to a higher standard of education for Arkansas teachers.[271]

The council would conduct the College Conference on Economic Education, which was attended by economists and educators from around the state. The conference was designed to share approaches for teaching economics at the college level and opportunities for economic education specialization in teacher education institutions. The colleges also sent staff members to participate in the council's 1964 summer workshops.[272]

Arkansas State Teachers College (ASTC, now UCA) in Conway got an $8,000 grant from the National Committee for Education in Family Finance in March 1965, which provided a program in both family economics and social economics. Robert Gibson, executive secretary of the organization, said that Arkansas had shown such interest in the economics program that the committee had passed over eighty-seven other educational institutions to give the grant to ASTC. Gibson also said that Arch Ford and Bessie Moore had influenced the committee to select Arkansas. For the previous two years, Moore had sought to interest the organization in Arkansas. The grant presentation was made in the office of Commissioner Ford.[273]

In 1967, the Arkansas Council on Economic Education got a grant to produce an economic education television series for the state of Arkansas. This was the first of its kind in the nation. Dr. Charles Venus, a young economist on the staff of the University of Arkansas Industrial Research and Extension Center, was the host of this new series. Venus used costumes for skits, and he created a character named Mr. Inflation to teach economics in an interesting way. There were sixty-five lessons in the series. The half-hour programs were broadcast around the state at 6:30 a.m. during the school year for about five years. The tapes were also circulated among the other educational television networks in surrounding states.[274] The council would go on to produce other economic education television programs and participate in other economic education television productions.

Number One in Economic Education

By the mid-1960s, Arkansas was becoming known as a leading state in economic education. Dr. Bessie Moore and Dr. George Fersh were invited to the Southern Governors' Conference in August 1963 to share their story of success in the Arkansas economic education program. Moore, the first women ever to address a session of the conference, gave a speech titled, "Arkansas Reacts to a Positive Program of Economics."[275]

In early 1966, the Little Rock School District was chosen as one of twenty-nine districts to be part of a Joint Council on Economic Education experiment called the Developmental Economic Education Program (DEEP). The program would develop economic curriculum for all twelve grades. Little Rock was chosen because of the positive reputation both the council and the Little Rock School District had gained in developing economic education. "We would not be knocking at your door if it were not for the fact that we have such high regard for the Little Rock School System," said Dr. M. L. Frankel, executive director of the Joint Council.

Little Rock hired a full-time coordinator of economic education for the program. Four Arkansas colleges—the University of Arkansas, Henderson State Teachers College, Little Rock University, and Arkansas State Teachers College—offered to assist with the program. The Arkansas Department of Education agreed to allow its supervisory staff to help, and Arch Ford agreed to publish the curriculum materials and distribute them throughout the state. Winthrop Rockefeller and several other businessmen helped pay the expenses of the program.[276]

Dr. Lewis Webster Jones, the chair and CEO of the Joint Council, later spoke at the annual meeting of the Arkansas Council on Economic Education. He praised the Arkansas program and said that the council was "by all odds the best in the country."[277]

In 1966, just four years after the Arkansas Council on Economic Education was founded, Arkansas was recognized by the Calvin K. Kazanjian Economics Foundation as being the number-one state for economic education. Of the forty awards presented nationally for excellence in teaching economics, ten were given to Arkansas teachers. The Kazanjian Foundation was established by the founder of Mounds Candy Company, and he established the Kazanjian Awards to encourage the teaching of economic principles.[278] The next year, Arkansas again led the nation in the Kazanjian Awards. Arkansas teachers received eighteen of the fifty-three awards given.[279]

Arch Ford also gained recognition for his role in economic education. In 1964, he was presented with the Award for Educators by the Freedom Foundation for his role in economic education. He was elected to be on the board of directors for the Joint Council on Economic Education in 1965. He was reelected to serve additional three-year terms, in 1968, 1971, and 1974. At the Joint Council meeting in 1968, the Arkansas Council on Economic Education was named as one of only five state councils whose programs were given "plus ratings" (the highest rating given by the Joint Council).[280]

Growing Economic Education

When the Arkansas Council on Economic Education was established in 1962, there were twenty-six contributors from twelve counties who were supporting economic education. By 1971, there were 834 contributors from seventy-three counties. By 1977, more than $100,000 was raised annually from the private sector. Some 1,200 business firms, individuals, associations, labor unions, and

FREEDOMS FOUNDATION AWARDS

A special and gratifying event of the University of Arkansas Summer—1964 Economic Education Workshops Banquet was the presentation of two Freedoms Foundation Awards. Gen. G. S. Meloy, Jr., General U.S.A. (Retired), Regional Vice President, Freedoms Foundation, Valley Forge, Pennsylvania, presented these awards:

Economic Education Award:
> Economic Education Workshop of Arkansas—1963

Educator's Award:
> Dr. A. W. Ford, Arkansas Commissioner of Education

OTHER AWARDS OF HONOR

Kept as closely guarded secrets until their presentation at the Banquet, special awards in recognition of meritorious service were received and deeply appreciated by Dr. Bessie B. Moore and Dr. George L. Fersh.

Winthrop Rockefeller, one of Arkansas' best known citizens and an ardent supporter of Education in his state, congratulates Dr. Arch W. Ford for his Educator's Award from the Freedoms Foundation.

Dr. Arch W. Ford is the proud and happy recipient of the Freedoms Foundation's Educator's Award. The Arkansas Commissioner of Education received the Award from Gen. G. S. Meloy, Jr., Regional Vice President of the Freedoms Foundation, in recognition of Dr. Ford's contribution toward a better understanding and a greater appreciation of the American Way of Life. Left to right: Gen. Meloy, Dr. Ford, and Dr. George L. Fersh.

In 1964, the Freedoms Foundation at Valley Forge, Pennsylvania, awarded Arch Ford the Freedoms Foundation's educators' award. The Arkansas Council on Economic Education also received the Economic Education Award for the 1963 UALR economic education workshop. *Photo courtesy of Economics Arkansas*

farm groups contributed sums from $10 to $1,500. The Department of Education also increased its contributions to $40,000 by 1977.[281]

Contributors were reminded of the work of the council through a series of 100 billboards erected throughout Arkansas during the months that economic education workshops were in progress. The signs, courtesy of Baird Advertising Company of Little Rock, said, "Economic Education is Working in Arkansas—Your Financial Support is Important." Miniature billboards were given to business leaders to keep on their desks so they would be reminded to contribute.[282]

Other procedures were put in place to strengthen and grow the organization. Orientation sessions were held for new council members to help them understand their roles in achieving the aims of the organization. Conferences for college instructors were held to expand

and strengthen the participation of the state's colleges in economic education. The council brought in some of the finest experts in the field as well as teachers who could demonstrate practical strategies for teaching economics in the classroom. A third strategy was to draw attention to the program through an awards luncheon for the teachers who had won national awards in economic education during the previous year.[283] When, in 1973, the Kazanjian Foundation decided not to sponsor the national awards anymore, International Paper Corporation picked up the sponsorship.

In 1972, the Arkansas Council on Economic Education celebrated its tenth anniversary. Arch Ford spoke at the event. He said: "In my opinion, the greatest threat to the private enterprise system in America is the lack of basic understanding of its purpose and way of functioning. To lessen this threat, the Department of Education's part in the economic education program in Arkansas has been one of sustained and wholehearted support, cooperation and persistence in turning a problem into an educational opportunity for teaching students how to think about economics in an orderly, rational way. Whatever leadership and encouragement I have been able to offer in this direction has been strengthened by the Department of Education staff, school administrators, supervisors, teachers and overall business community."

Representative Wilbur Mills speaking at a 1969 economic education luncheon. Arch Ford is seated beside the podium.
Photo courtesy of Economics Arkansas

By this time, the council had won the Freedoms Foundation Award five times and both Arch Ford and Bessie Moore had won the Valley Forge Schoolman's Award for their role in leading the development of economic education.[284]

Business/Education Partnership

"In my opinion, the greatest threat to the private enterprise system in America is the lack of basic understanding of its purpose and way of functioning.

"To lessen this threat, the Department of Education's part in the economic education program in Arkansas has been one of sustained and wholehearted support, cooperation and persistence in turning a problem into an educational opportunity for teaching students how to think about economics in an orderly, rational way.

"Whatever leadership and encouragement I have been able to offer in this direction has been strengthened by the Department of Education staff, school administrators, supervisors, teachers, and the overall business community."

DR. A. W. FORD
Director of Education

"There is a special excitement in our 10th Anniversary! In ten short years, Arkansas has become recognized as Number 1 in the innovative teaching of economics and in the sharing of these new learning concepts. Equally as thrilling to me is the broad-based support that has made this dramatic rise to excellence possible. Many individuals, companies and organizations throughout the State have been most generous with their money and time dedicated to helping our young people make better decisions in their personal lives and as voters in our democratic system. Our school administrators and teachers have caught the spirit of this exciting new program. To all, we are most grateful."

DR. BESSIE B. MOORE
Coordinator of the Program

Official statements from Arch Ford and Bessie Moore in the program for the 10th anniversary of the Arkansas Council on Economic Education in 1972. *Photo courtesy of Economics Arkansas*

Economic Education Centers

Arkansas continued to lead the nation in economic education. The Arkansas Council on Economic Education started establishing economic education centers on Arkansas college campuses beginning in 1969, with the first one at Henderson State College. The M. H. Russell Center for Economic Education, named after Henderson's president, was set up to better assist teachers in obtaining resources to teach economics. Russell, a past president of the Arkansas Council, was nationally known for his leadership in economic education in the state.[285] In 1979, the Bessie Boehm Moore Center for Economic Education would be established on the University of Arkansas campus. It was a fitting tribute for the dynamo who had been selected by Arch Ford to get an economic education program up and running in Arkansas. The council also created the Bessie B. Moore Economic Education Awards, a state awards program to honor excellence in teaching economics. The Arkansas Council, now known as Economics Arkansas, is still conducting workshops and promoting economic education in Arkansas today.

The Legacy

Joe Ford's wish for a high school economics class resulted in a wonderful program that has assisted many Arkansas teachers at all grade levels in teaching economic education. Conway High School,

Arch Ford speaking at the 1977 Arkansas Council on Economic Education luncheon. *Photo courtesy of Arch Ford Collection, UA Special Collections*

Joe's alma mater, created a high school economics class which was an elective class until the state mandated a required high school economics class starting in 2014.

Chapter 9: Educational Television in Arkansas

With the development of television, the Arkansas Department of Education began to envision a way to improve education for all Arkansas students through the use of educational television programs. On June 4, 1954, the Arkansas Educational Television Association was created to "furnish non-profit and non-commercial educational television broadcast services to the State of Arkansas."[286] The group mostly focused on providing educational television through the commercial channels that were broadcasting in the state.

In July 1958, Commissioner Arch Ford named a steering committee for developing educational television programs. The twenty-five-member steering committee was made up of state legislators, college presidents, Department of Education staff members, Arkansas Education Association representatives, the director of the Arkansas Children's Colony, and representatives from the Arkansas Committee on Television Affairs—which had members from KATV, KTHV, KARK, and the regional television stations.[287]

In 1959, the Arkansas General Assembly began a two-year legislative study on the state's need for educational television. The study resulted in the introduction of a bill in the 1961 legislative session. The bill became Act 198 (1961), which created the Arkansas Educational Television Commission. The commission was "to provide instructional, educational television for schools and the general public...and to help with the preservation of the public peace, health and safety."[288]

Just as the perceived threat of communism resulted in the development of the Arkansas Council on Economic Education,

it also influenced the creation of educational television in
Arkansas. The act stated, "Young people of the state...are the chief
objects of brainwashing operations engineered by the minions of
totalitarianism....Countermeasures to such subversive influences are
necessary to the continued existence of constitutional democracy."[289]

Arkansas Educational Television Commission

The first meeting of the Arkansas Educational Television (known
as ETV) Commission was held March 1, 1962, in the Department
of Education building. Eight commissioners had been chosen by
Governor Orval Faubus to serve a seven-year term. Each commissioner
was selected to represent a particular interest group. The ETV
commissioners represented public education, higher education,
the four U.S. congressional districts, women, and minorities. The
commission would meet regularly on a quarterly basis.[290]

T. E. Tyler of Little Rock, a former Pulaski County state representative,
was chosen to be the first chairman of the ETV Commission. C. C. Gibson
Jr. of Jerome was elected vice-chairman, while Mrs. O. P. Hammons of
Forrest City was elected secretary. Heloise Griffon, the supervisor of
audio-visual services for the Department of Education, would also be
working with the commission. The commission also voted to ask the
Federal Communications Commission (FCC) for title to the educational
television channels in Little Rock, Fort Smith, and Fayetteville.[291] These
channels would become part of the new Arkansas Educational Television
Network (AETN).

Later in March, Tyler announced that the state was setting up a
statewide television network through stations in three areas. He also
announced that the commission would be asking the FCC to transfer
Channel 14 from Stuttgart to Jonesboro. That would give the network
four channels: Channel 2/Little Rock, Channel 13/Fayetteville,
Channel 14/Jonesboro, and Channel 16/Fort Smith. Tyler said that
the commission would later ask the FCC to move Channel 16 to

southwestern Arkansas to improve coverage in the state.

Tyler also announced a deal with KATV-7, which had offered to give AETN its facilities in Jefferson Springs (later Redfield). These facilities included a tower, a building, a transmission line, and eighty acres of land worth $175,000, contingent on the FCC's approval for KATV to establish new transmitting facilities in Little Rock. The Arkansas legislature had appropriated funds for the network in the 1963 session, and matching federal funds would be available to try to have the network on the air sometime in 1963.[292]

The ETV Commission set up guidelines for AETN programming. The stated primary objective of the network was "that of supplementing academic education facilities for adults in the state of Arkansas," and the commission also "accepts an obligation to present cultural programs for the enlightenment and enjoyment of the public." The guidelines further stated that the commission did not consider itself obligated to "air controversial matters nor to provide a forum for the expounding of ideologies of any group body or agency." It decided that public affairs programming should be confined to programs that had a dialogue or debate format so that both sides of an issue could be presented. The commission also wanted to present programming that had strong moral values. It prohibited the showing of programs that contained vulgarities or obscenities.[293]

Starting the Arkansas Educational Television Network

The 1963 Arkansas General Assembly appropriated funds to the get the network up and running. It appropriated $250,000 in matching funds for the next biennium, which included a $14,000 salary for a director and $10,000 salaries for the program manager and chief engineer to be hired for the network. The act authorized the network to hire twenty-nine employees. Although opponents said the state could not afford it, the "Old Guard" in the House of Representatives led the fight for the passage of the legislation. Legislation was also passed to fund the operation of the ETV Commission for the next biennium. It received $16,000 a year for operating expenses.[294]

A total of $63,500 was appropriated for broadcast operations for the 1963-64 fiscal year and $157,000 for the 1964-65 fiscal year. The legislature also appropriated $150,000 for the construction and up to $100,000 for the maintenance of a new studio to be built in Conway. It was announced that the network would operate only during the hours that children were in school. It would broadcast instruction in subjects that schools indicated were needed and was intended to supplement the teachers' instruction. Later on, the network could possibly expand to a ten-hour day and provide adult education courses.[295]

Lee Reeves, dean at Arkansas Agricultural and Mechanical College (Arkansas A&M—now the University of Arkansas at Monticello), was chosen by the commission in April 1963 to be the first director of AETN. He had been superintendent of Hermitage Schools for fifteen years and had been a senator from Bradley County for sixteen years.[296] Federal funds came through in June 1963, so educational television was on its way to becoming a reality. The commission applied to the FCC for an operation permit in April 1963, and the target date for getting the network on the air was set for July 1, 1964.[297]

Political Troubles

In the summer of 1963, Commissioner Ford had to step in to defend the ETV Commission. Critics said that there was no justification for the creation of a separate commission to oversee educational television in the state, suggesting instead that the program be put under the state Board of Education. Ford responded by saying, "The General Assembly has pursued the traditional pattern in Arkansas by providing for a separate commission and thus making possible a speedy development of the program. You will recall that the same approach was made in establishing the Arkansas Children's Colony, the Boys and Girls Training Schools, the state Library Commission and the Blind and Deaf Schools." He said the reason these were established under separate commissions, rather than under the Board of Education, was to permit each to develop as quickly as possible. He said that he mentioned this because the reasons had not yet been publicly stated. He also stated that the Board of Education could not possibly have the time to devote to the educational television program because it was charged with the management of a $60 million public school fund. Educational television would not get the attention that it needed.[298]

Ford named Dean H. Whiteside, director of instructional services at the Department of Education, to be a coordinator of the ETV Commission. Ford told T. E. Tyler, chairman of the ETV Commission, that the department would assist the new commission and that Whiteside would help establish a suitable educational television program to be tied to the curriculum in the public schools.[299] In 1971, however, the ETV Commission would be put under the Department of Education as part of Governor Dale Bumpers's reorganization of state government.

On the Air

AETN did not meet the earlier target date set by the ETV Commission in 1963. In addition to the tower that the network received from KATV, three other towers needed to be built across Arkansas. The plans were to build a Channel 13 tower for northwestern Arkansas at Pettigrew, while the Channel 9 tower for southwestern Arkansas would be built at Prescott. A tower for Channel 9 in southeastern Arkansas would be built at Strawberry.[300]

Funds for building the AETN broadcasting studio were not released until 1965, and construction bids were not awarded until early 1966. Nabholz Construction of Conway was awarded the bid to build the $294,530 AETN station facility, which would be located in Conway

The original Arkansas Educational Television Network studios in Conway, Arkansas. *Photo courtesy of Jess Setzler, AETN Marketing and Outreach*

on the campus of what was known at that time as State College of Arkansas (SCA); it became the University of Central Arkansas (UCA) in 1975. SCA granted the ETV Commission a ninety-nine-year lease on a three-acre tract of land that was adjacent to the main campus. Little Rock legislators had wanted the facility to be built in Little Rock, but Senator Guy "Mutt" Jones of Conway, a member of the "Old Guard," won out and Conway was selected. The Conway City Council provided $61,000 to pay for the microwave relay system that was necessary to send the signal from Conway to the educational TV tower in Redfield, which was about forty-five miles away. The Conway Area Chamber of Commerce also provided $3,852 in funding for the new studio.[301] The street running beside the studio would be named Sesame Street.

In March 1966, a new target date was set for getting the network on the air. Lee Reeves, AETN's director, said he wanted to see the network on the air by October 1, 1966. That was contingent on the construction of the towers and on the station at Conway being completed within six months. It would take two months to install the equipment. The new network would operate on UHF (ultra-high frequency) Channel 2 with 400,000 watts of power. Because of the high frequency, the channel had a shorter broadcast range, and signals could not go through or around big objects like buildings or mountains.[302] The October deadline was not met either. The station finally went on the air December 4, 1966. Eventually the legislature would appropriate the funds to get stations at Arkadelphia and Fayetteville up and running.

Early Educational Programming

In its first years of operation, KETS Channel 2 was associated with National Educational Television, which preceded the Public Broadcasting System (PBS). Broadcasts were in black and white, and the focus was primarily on instructional programming for use in Arkansas classrooms.

AETN received educational programs from other educational television stations through either telephone lines or through the mail.[303] AETN also shared some of the programs created in Arkansas with other stations through these methods. Eventually the broadcast day would be expanded and the station would operate seven days a week instead of five.

In September 1967, Arch Ford began to appear in a weekly program on AETN called "A Visit with the Commissioner." It was broadcast at 7:30 p.m. every Tuesday evening. He discussed various educational issues in an effort to keep the public informed about what was going on in Arkansas education.

Following a program on November 4, Commissioner Ford received a letter from Dr. Cecil McDermott of Hendrix College in Conway. McDermott wrote in the letter, "The program was excellent in content and spoke to some very major issues. Your experience provides you with the knowledge to quickly evaluate new trends in light of your own personal well-defined philosophy of education. Some, 'many,' educators do not have a reference point—a belief about what is 'good education.' Ask many leading educators a question and they must consider the audience, the politics, etc. You consider these but only in light of a well thought out experience oriented philosophy."[304]

After a March 1975 program, Ford received a letter from former governor Sid McMath. McMath said, "As I watched you field these questions and answer them frankly and honestly and with the accumulated wisdom that comes only with experience, I reviewed in my mind's eye the turbulent history of education in Arkansas and the tremendous contribution which you have made. You have indeed been a good and faithful servant and I know of no one that has made a greater contribution than you have toward improving the educational opportunities of our Arkansas children—black and white, rich and poor."[305]

Arkansas children were treated to a daily dose of entertaining educational children's programming through AETN beginning in the late 1960s. The first episode of *Mister Rogers' Neighborhood* aired nationally on public television for the first time on February 19, 1968. Created by Fred Rogers, it was aimed at two- to five-year-olds and covered a broad range of topics through visits to the "world of make believe." The first episode of *Sesame Street* aired on November 10, 1969. Created by the Children's Television Network (CTW), the program used such characters as Big Bird, Bert and Ernie, and Cookie Monster to teach the alphabet, colors, and numbers to young viewers. CTW built on its success from *Sesame Street* to then produce *The Electric Company*, which aired for the first time on October 21, 1971. Targeting children ages six to ten, it taught basic reading and grammar skills through skits and songs. CTW also published a biweekly teacher's guide for these programs.

In Living Color

AETN began the move to color programming in February 1972 when a horn antenna was installed on top of the microwave platform on the Southwestern Bell Building in Little Rock. The antenna would beam the PBS signal to a relay station at High Point, north of Roland, where a 300-foot tower had been built. The signal was then strengthened and relayed to a thirty-seven-foot tower on Cadron Ridge, west of Conway, for relay to the KETS transmitter.[306]

The state legislature appropriated funds for color transmission from the station at that time but not for originating programs in color. The station would have to get matching funds from the federal government before the equipment could be purchased. Although this technological arrangement was awkward, it allowed KETS to begin telecasting PBS network programs in color on April 2, 1972.[307] Legislative appropriations in the 1973-74 and 1974-75 fiscal years would allow AETN to convert to full color programming.

One immediate advantage was that *Sesame Street, The Electric Company*, and *Mister Rogers' Neighborhood* could be carried locally at the time they were broadcast nationally. Before this change, KETS had to get videotapes of PBS programs through the mail. The shows would have to be aired a week later. Arkansans could now also see some of the PBS news programs that they were not able to see before because PBS had not allowed them to be run later.[308]

Expanding Services

The ETV Commission was transferred to the Department of Education in 1971 under Governor Dale Bumpers's reorganization of state government agencies. It was allowed to keep all its statutory powers—including rule-making and settling disputes—but the governor was given the power to review the rules, standards, and regulations devised by the commission and veto them if he chose to do so. The governor could also dismiss the head of the commission. The commissioner of education (Arch Ford at this time) would handle the budgeting, purchasing, and "related management functions" of the agency. Since the Department of Education had to get its budget approved and recommended by the state Board of Education, this meant that most financial requests from AETN could be included in the Department of Education budget.[309]

In 1973, the Arkansas General Assembly appropriated state funds to convert AETN to full color programming and to build three new transmitters. It authorized the building of a fourth transmitter if revenues permitted. The federal government provided about $2.3 million to build the new transmitters.[310] AETN at that time had only one transmitter at the tower in Redfield, with a transmission radius of eighty-five miles. The station had been sending programming to about forty counties or parts of counties, but some of them were receiving services through cable. Since cable was only available in the larger cities, this meant that the rural school districts that needed educational television did not have access to it.

The three transmitters were installed, which allowed three more stations to go online at the end of 1976 and in early 1977. KETG/Channel 9 in Arkadelphia went online October 29, 1976, providing services to southwestern Arkansas, while KAFT/Channel 13 in Fayetteville went online December 9, 1976, providing services to northwestern Arkansas. KTEJ/Channel 19 began transmitting January 13, 1977, providing services to northeastern Arkansas. The fourth station, KEMV/Channel 6 in Mountain View, would not go online until June 21, 1980. When that took place, AETN would finally provide coverage to over 90% of the state.[311] (Bureaucratic bungling at the federal level was said to be the cause of the delayed construction of the Mountain View station.)

Satellite Feed

In February 1978, KETS began receiving all its PBS programs from

Western Union's Westar II satellite. PBS was the first entity in the world to deliver its programming by satellite transmission. Although this was on an experimental basis, it would be the beginning of a much better way to receive programming. The test also demonstrated better audio and video quality. By this time, PBS programs made up the bulk of evening programming. The Westar II satellite, parked in an orbit 22,300 miles high, increased the number of programs that could be transmitted to AETN simultaneously. The station could now choose between different programs being transmitted. This also allowed the network to tape two programs at a time or tape one and broadcast another at the same time.[312]

This new technology would cut down on the cost of transmitting programs around the state. The network used UHF channels, which have a smaller range than VHF channels. Microwave centers had to be set up every thirty miles so that the signals could be transmitted. The weakened signal was strengthened at each station before it was sent off to the next one. The power cost of all this was continually increasing. Another problem was finding maintenance workers who could keep the system up and running. The salary for the position was only $10,000, however, so people with those skills could often make more money somewhere else.[313]

Fundraising

Most AETN viewers are familiar with the periodic fundraising campaigns that are undertaken. Banks of phone volunteers waiting to take donations are a familiar sight during these campaigns. The first time the network turned to the public for funds to support programming was in 1978. AETN participated in the PBS "Festival 98," offering days of specials designed to attract public attention and funds.[314] The AETN Foundation, made up of the eight commissioners and seven at-large elected lay members, would be established in 1984 to conduct all the fundraising for the network. The Friends of AETN would later be set up as a volunteer and public relations support organization for the network. It became the face of fundraising for the network.[315]

AETN continued to expand and change after Arch Ford retired. The station at Conway doubled in size in the late 1990s and now has four production studios and a modern technical center. In the first decade of the twenty-first century, the network made the switch from analog to digital signals. It has three channels, AETN-PBS, AETN-Create, and AETN PLUS. It also provides an audio-only reading service on AETN-4 for the blind. It also launched "Arkansas IDEAs" (Internet Delivered Education for Arkansas Schools) to provide high-quality, standards-based professional development offerings, online programming, and instructional resources to K-12 educators in Arkansas.[316]

Chapter 10: Educating Children with Disabilities

A rkansas was a little slower than most states in establishing programs to serve students with mental and physical disabilities, but once the state started on the path to educating these students, it quickly gained national attention in this area. Until 1959, the only state-sponsored service for children with disabilities was either the State Hospital, which was for patients with intellectual disabilities, or one of the four reform schools. This care was, for the most part, custodial. State Hospital administrators constantly protested the placement of children and adults who at that time were called "feebleminded," arguing that they were not equipped to deal with such cases.[317]

At that time, the State Hospital was a horrific place to be because of the lack of funding. There were some 5,000 patients there, but some patients were sleeping on the floor because of the shortage of beds. The superintendent had to scrounge for everything. One story was that he acquired a load of Ku Klux Klan costumes and had the female patients sew them into bedsheets. Legislators who inspected the place found conditions so deplorable that they frequently became ill. Governor Orval Faubus became aware of these conditions early in his first term and got the legislature to appropriate funds for its improvement. The hospital was given new buildings, more medicines, additional staff members with better training, and improved programs.[318]

Establishment of the Arkansas Children's Colony

During his first weeks in office, Governor Faubus also spoke out in support of a pilot residential school for children with intellectual

disabilities. With his backing, the legislature overwhelmingly passed
Act 6 of 1955, which authorized the governor to appoint a board of
directors for the prospective Arkansas Children's Colony (now called
the Conway Human Development Center). A modest appropriation
allowed the board to research colony designs and to search for an
executive director. Faubus appointed Nils Florentz, whose daughter
had intellectual disabilities, to be chairman of the board. Florentz
had begun crusading in the late 1940s for more special education
classes in local schools and to establish a publicly funded "colony" for
those with intellectual and cognitive disabilities in Arkansas. Keith
Tudor of Arkadelphia, a Faubus campaign supporter who had shared
with Faubus his struggles of raising a child with disabilities, was also
named a board member.[319]

David Ray was appointed as the first director of the Arkansas
Children's Colony in January 1957. He had been executive director
of the Arizona Society for Crippled Children and Adults, but he
also had experience as assistant director of the New Iowa Hospital
School for the Handicapped. The Iowa school had made important
innovations in special education.[320] The legislature appropriated $1.6
million for the next biennium to build and operate the colony.

The design of the new institution would be different from most
of the multi-story facilities that were being used at the time. Eight
small, one-story dormitories would be arranged like a small village.
Each cottage would have two bedrooms and a total of thirty-two beds.
At that time, there would be space for a total of 256 children in the
facility.[321]

Faubus selected Conway as the location for the colony after
considering seventy possible sites in twelve counties. The city
agreed to donate a 405-acre site and to provide utility lines without
charge. One of the advantages of the Conway site was the possibility
of collaborating with Arkansas State Teachers College (now the

University of Central Arkansas) to teach the colony residents and to provide a practicum site for special education students from the college. Nabholz Construction Company of Conway was selected to build the first buildings.[322]

The program that was developed ranged from a preschool experience for younger children to academic instruction, vocational training, and social development for older children. The goal was for each child to "become an active, participating member of his society." It was emphasized that the new colony would be an educational institution, not a custodial one. The children would also be able to participate in scouting, religious activities, intramural softball, bicycling, fishing, bus rides, and games. Teachers would emphasize "learning by doing," allowing each child to "proceed at his own rate until he has reached his fullest development."[323]

The first children moved in on September 1, 1959. David Ray and the board decided to first admit children with mild intellectual delays, despite his belief that such children should receive local public education. They did this in order to demonstrate to the Arkansas Department of Education and the local school districts that special education was feasible and practical. Ray told members of the Conway Rotary Club that first preference for admission would be school-age and educable children and that custodial care of children and adults with severe intellectual disabilities was a later goal. He envisioned that most of the original colony residents would eventually be able to enter public schools.

Dedication services were held on October 4, 1959. About 3,000 people attended the opening ceremony. J. Thomas McIntire, superintendent of the Arizona Children's Colony who served as a consultant, told Arkansans who attended the ceremony, "Right now, your state is in advance of many states that have had institutions for years." Within a year, the Canadian Association for Retarded

Children ranked the Arkansas Children's Colony as one of the best facilities for children with mental disabilities in the United States. South Carolina and Oklahoma would adopt the Arkansas model for their new facilities.[324]

An Advocate for Special Education

Even before Arkansas established the Children's Colony, there were those who were advocating that special education services be provided by the public schools. In 1955, the Arkansas Crippled Children's Association joined forces with the state Department of Education and the University of Arkansas to sponsor a workshop for training public school teachers and administrators in methods of classroom instruction for children with intellectual and physical disabilities. The children who participated in the workshop were recruited from around Washington County. It was hoped that there would eventually be permanent courses at the college level to train teachers, as there were children in every county in Arkansas who could be taught at these training facilities. Educators also planned for the Arkansas Children's Colony to be a place where educational training could take place and teachers could serve in internships.[325]

In the first significant federal action for special education, the U.S. Congress appropriated $675,000 in 1957 for research in special education. The Council of State Governments recommended in 1958 that states mandate education for children with retardation and subsidize local special education classes.[326]

Although the colony was lauded for its architectural design and model curriculum, probably its greatest impact was that it gave its director, David Ray, a platform for advocating special education in the public schools. Everywhere he spoke, he advocated the need for more comprehensive services for those with intellectual disabilities. He believed that most children with these disabilities did not need to be institutionalized but needed to be provided local special education classes. He argued that a state-sponsored residential school should exist for only those children whose needs could not be met by the local schools. He said that the colony would work toward an "enriched curriculum in Arkansas' public schools, special classes and even special schools in the larger cities, home training and vocational training."[327]

Ray often recruited support to further his message. Twice he invited Gunnar Dybwad, executive director of the National Association for Retarded Children (now known as the Arc), to Arkansas to challenge the state to do more for children with intellectual disabilities. Dybwad in 1958 said that most children did not need to be institutionalized and that parents should advocate for public special education classes. During his 1960 visit, he praised the colony but said the state should create "classes for the less seriously retarded in the public schools" and "training and facilities for retarded adults to earn part of their own way."[328]

In 1960, Ray was speaking at a conference on the needs for special education and rehabilitation in the South when he was approached by Eunice Shriver, sister to John F. Kennedy, who said she would like to visit the colony. Shriver had developed a real passion for those with developmental disabilities as a result of her experience in taking care of her older sister.

David Ray, director of the Arkansas Children's Colony, escorts Eunice Shriver (sister of John F. Kennedy) on a tour of the facility in May 1963. *Photo courtesy of UCA Archives*

The oldest Kennedy sister, Rosemary, had suffered some developmental delays since her birth in 1918. Her father, Joe Kennedy, who said he wanted her to have a more "normal" life, took his twenty-three-year-old daughter to George

Washington University Hospital for an experimental procedure, a lobotomy. The procedure robbed her of many of the physical and cognitive capabilities that she had had previously, and she was institutionalized in a Catholic Church-run facility. She lived there until her death in 2005 at age eighty-six. The family was told that visiting her would "upset" her, so it was not until the 1960s that her siblings began to visit her. Eunice would eventually assume responsibility for her care.

Eunice Shriver finally came to Arkansas in May 1963 to speak to the Arkansas Association for Retarded Children. She took a tour of the colony and had high praise for it, not only for the facility but for the research on special education that was being done there. She predicted that Arkansas could be the leading state in research on mental disabilities.[329]

A few weeks later, Shriver asked Ray to come to Washington DC to lend a hand in getting federal legislation passed regarding intellectual disabilities. Representative Oren Harris of Arkansas introduced the legislation, written by the President's Panel on Mental Retardation, to fund research on intellectual disabilities. The centerpiece of the legislation was a proposal to give grants to states to develop comprehensive plans for developmental disabilities services. The Maternal and Child Health and Mental Retardation Planning Amendments (Public Law 88-156) were passed, and Ray attended the ceremony in the Oval Office when President Kennedy signed the bill.[330] After President Kennedy's assassination, Ray took a job with the Kennedy Foundation so that he could continue to promote special education.[331]

Special Education in Arkansas Public Schools

Back in Arkansas, Arch Ford had taken up the cause for special education. In a school administrators' meeting in February 1961, he said that special education needed to be guided in a different direction.

He warned that "unless public schools accept the responsibility for the education of exceptional children, non-educational agencies will secure the funds and undertake the tasks." He said that the parents and friends of these children would find *someone* to educate them, and he cautioned that the educational program could go off in many directions and lack the unity of purpose and direction it should have."[332]

The next year, the state Department of Education conducted a special census in fourteen school districts to find out how many people aged one to twenty-one in the state had special needs. Fourteen districts were chosen because Commissioner Ford had decided to sample a cross section of Arkansas's 417 districts to determine whether the reported national average applied to Arkansas. About 3,000 of the 27,112 children in the fourteen districts were found to have some disability. Based on this sample, it was believed that 45,000 youth in Arkansas had special needs. Department specialists believed that 90-95% of these children could be educated in the public schools.[333]

The Arkansas Legislative Council was also interested in knowing how prevalent intellectual disabilities were in children in the state. Its research department released a report in March 1962 saying that three out of every ten children born in the state had intellectual disabilities. Children with these challenges were receiving little or no regular public schooling at that time. Of those children who were ages six to eighteen, it was estimated that 8,000 were considered educable (IQ 50-75), 3,000 were considered trainable (IQ 25-50), and 1,000 were totally dependent with no measurable IQ. The report showed that public and private enterprises were providing some education and training for 1,128 of the educable children and for 342 of the trainable children, but little or no care was available for totally dependent children except those who were institutionalized.[334]

The report also surveyed what other states were doing and what services Arkansas was currently providing for these children. The report showed that other states seemed to be taking care of more adults than children and that care seemed to be more custodial than educational. Arkansas had the following eight institutions or programs available at the time for those with intellectual disabilities:

1) The Arkansas Children's Colony, which was serving 320 clients. Construction was under way to increase that to 540. There was a waiting list of more than 1,500.

2) The State Hospital, which had about 1,100 patients with intellectual disabilities. About 92 of those were children who were housed in a special cottage.

3) The School for the Blind, which accepted children who could make some progress and whose presence did not affect the progress of the typically abled child.

4) The School for the Deaf, which carried on a limited multiple-disabilities program with 29 deaf children with intellectual disabilities.

5) The Department of Education reported that there were 79 special classes for children with intellectual and physical disabilities, but at least 500 were needed. There were more than 10 private classes for children considered trainable. The state gave $100 per child per year to school districts to cover the excess cost of education for the children with intellectual disabilities in their home communities. The districts also received $200 a schoolyear for educating those with physical disabilities.

6) The Health Department had general planning, protection, and operation of services to those with intellectual disabilities as well as allied clinical and diagnostic counseling.

7) The Welfare Department reported that there were about 75 children with intellectual disabilities in foster care. These children received aid because they were neglected, dependent, or delinquent.

8) The Vocational Rehabilitation Service reported that it treated

developmental/intellectual disabilities, but the individual had to be at least sixteen years old and considered educable. The Rehabilitation Service also worked with the Arkansas Children's Colony, the State Hospital, and other public and private agencies.[335]

The state Board of Education reviewed these reports and made concerted efforts over the next year to improve services for those with intellectual disabilities. In a January 1963 report on the state's progress in education, Arch Ford said that modest strides had been made in the program for "handicapped and exceptional" children. In-service training for teachers was implemented through expanded state college offerings, workshops, and other kinds of professional development. Act 331 of 1961 had provided more facilities for those with severe disabilities and Act 337 of 1961 had provided funding for UAMS to do research on children who had minimal brain damage.[336]

Progress was slow, but the state Board of Education adopted a plan in 1967 to try to reach more special needs students. Tom Hicks, supervisor for special education in the Department of Education, said that only 6,033 of the 66,597 identified students with disabilities had been served the previous year. The plan was to apply for about $400,000 in federal aid under Title VI of the Elementary and Secondary Education Act (ESEA). Title VI was an incentive program to encourage special education projects by the states. The federal government advanced $23,700 in a planning grant. Hicks said the present program was limited by lack of funds and trained people. He said the program would be available to both public and private schools. Commissioner Ford also announced at the meeting that he was creating the state Advisory Committee on Special Education. The organizational meeting for the advisory group would be held in late September 1967 in the former Highway Department building on the State Capitol grounds.[337]

The federal government did much to assist in the development of special education during the 1960s. The 1965 ESEA law had funded new special education programs for children with various disabilities. Public Law 89-3 provided additional federal support for state-sponsored schools. Congress also authorized financial aid to children with intellectual disabilities and expanded the special education provisions of ESEA in 1966. Congress passed PL 89-750, the Education of the Handicapped Act, in 1966, providing new federal grants for states to initiate, expand, and improve special education. It also established the National Advisory Committee on Handicapped Children as part of the Office of Education.

In 1967, Congress provided new funding for research in mental disabilities along with funding for physical education and recreation programs. In 1968, Congress enacted the Handicapped Children's Early Education Assistance Act to sponsor experimental early childhood education programs for children with disabilities. This was one of several programs that the federal government implemented in its attempt to expand its role in developmental disabilities services. New legislation also provided funds to help states implement the comprehensive plans that they drafted under Public Law 88-156, and Congress provided new funding for research and education and recreation programs. PL 91-230, and the Elementary, Secondary and Other Educational Amendments further stimulated states to develop special education programs.[338]

In 1969, Tom Hicks gave a report on the status of special education in the state. He said that 19.3% of the school population needed some kind of special education services. The number of special education classes had risen from 150 to 377 since he had taken the special education job at the Department of Education two years earlier, primarily because of increased federal aid. A total of 102 of the 364 districts in the state had at least one special education class, but there were a lot of children with disabilities in the state receiving no services at all. Of the 377 special education classes, 240 were for children considered educable, ten were for children considered trainable, forty-three were for children with speech delays, twenty-five were for children with learning disabilities, and seven were for children with physical disabilities. In Monticello, there was a class for children with emotional and behavioral disorders. There was also a class for the hearing impaired who were not qualified to attend the School for the Deaf. There were also 248 children who received homebound services in which a teacher came to the home and the state provided textbooks.[339]

The Department of Education's budget for special education in the 1969-70 school year was $451,000. The department was authorized to pay $200 per child or up to $2,000 per class to districts offering special education classes. The law setting that rate was passed in 1949 and had not been raised since. It also did not cover the teacher's salary any longer, as teachers' salaries had risen. Nor did it cover the cost of special materials or equipment that had been developed in the previous few years for use in special education classrooms. The result was that the maximum the department spent per class had decreased to about $1,580. The districts received Title I and Title VI funding from the federal government, but the rest of the cost had to be assumed by the district. Since the districts were not mandated to provide any services, the services and the money spent on them varied widely.[340]

The Arkansas Legislative Council held several hearings on public education and training programs for children with disabilities in July 1972. Commissioner Ford told the council that one in seven school-age children had some degree of disability, ranging from poor vision to more severe disabilities. The state by then maintained 520 special education programs for 12,000 children with intellectual disabilities. Ford said that that meant there were 80,000 to 90,000 students who were in need of some special assistance. He said the public schools should be responsible for the children who were classified as educable. That is why he was recommending that the state Board of Education ask for $2.5 million in the next biennium to start a mandatory public school program for all educable children with mental and other disabilities. Special education programs in 1962 were optional in Arkansas public schools, but the federal government was moving toward making special education mandatory.[341]

Dr. Ben N. Saltzman, president of the Arkansas Association for Retarded Children, reported to the council that there were about 16,700 "educable" children with disabilities in Arkansas, but only 5,160 were enrolled in public schools. He further stated that there were 2,066 "trainable" children with intellectual disabilities, but only 120 were enrolled in public schools. Dr. Roger Bost, director of the state's Department of Social and Rehabilitative Services, said that there were more federal funds available for education of those with disabilities in community centers than there were for educating them in the public schools. Arkansas had about 60 community centers at that time.[342]

Mandatory Special Education in Public Schools

In the 1973 legislative session, a law was passed mandating every district in the state to begin providing a full curriculum for children with disabilities by 1979. This was in anticipation of federal court decisions that would require the schools to serve this population. The legislature increased special education funding from $500,000 to $3.5 million by 1975.[343]

The state Department of Education rolled out its plan for special education in the public schools in January 1975. Roy Wood, coordinator of special education in the department, distributed the plans to the state's school districts for comment before the plan was sent to the legislature. The department, with the help of a California-based consulting firm, had been working on a plan for the schools to comply with the 1973 state law that required Arkansas schools to provide educational services equal to the regular school programs for all children with disabilities by 1979.[344]

Districts with a total average daily attendance of 4,000 were encouraged to set up a special education program that would provide a full array of services. Smaller districts could either join forces with other districts to start programs or they could contract with a nearby larger district to provide special education services. If there was a total average daily attendance of 4,000 among the districts that formed a consortium to provide services, the districts could hire a special education supervisor. Regional special education consultants from the Department of Education would be available to assist these districts in forming the consortium.[345]

Districts would be responsible for determining the number of children in need of special education and evaluating their learning challenges. They would then prepare their own plans for providing special education and submit those plans to the Department of Education. The state would have to approve those plans before reimbursing the districts with state funds.[346]

The department's plan outlined the following five services that should be part of each district's special education plan:

1) Itinerant instruction, in which a specialist serving more than one school works with children with disabilities and their teachers periodically in regular classrooms or special classes

2) Resource rooms where a specialist provides instruction for children with disabilities for short periods during the school day and works with regular teachers in planning instructional programs for children with disabilities in their classroom

3) Special classes that children with disabilities would attend for at least half a day, with the remainder of the day being spent in regular classes

4) Instruction at home or in hospitals for children whose health does not allow them to go to school

5) Programs in other agencies, such as the colony and the schools for the blind and deaf, when services cannot be obtained in public schools[347]

The department further stated that the goal of all special education programs would be to prepare children for regular classroom participation if possible. The department would establish guidelines for the districts to use in evaluating the kinds of services each child needed. The guidelines would include the requirement that the students be provided services in "the least restrictive setting" that was needed. The plan suggested that the curriculum for children with disabilities be the same as for typically abled children whenever possible. Children with disabilities would be guaranteed the same opportunities to take part in non-academic activities as other children. Districts would have to prepare an individual education plan (IEP) for each child receiving special education. The parents and the children would take part in developing the plan.[348]

The plan also called for districts to start providing special education for children who were below school age in cases in which the disabilities could become greater as time passed. This included hearing and visual impairments. The districts also needed to provide additional in-service training for teachers. Colleges would need to provide more graduate programs to train specialists and provide special training for regular classroom teachers. The legislature increased aid for special education from $3.5 million to $5 million in 1976 and $5.5 million in 1977.[349]

As expected, Congress passed the Education for All Handicapped

Children Act in 1975, which guaranteed free public education to children with disabilities. The law stated that children with mental and other disabilities were entitled to an education in the least restrictive environment. The Arkansas General Assembly began escalating funding to help districts comply with the law that required them to have an approved special education program by 1979.

For the 1975-76 school year, the legislature had appropriated $5 million, but collections were down just as the districts were adding more special education classrooms. The number of classrooms increased from 700 to almost 1,200, so the money had to be spread thinner. Another frustration was that districts that had been getting about $2.5 million under Title I of ESEA could no longer get those funds because the state was now mandating special education. Districts were already bearing about 60% of the cost of special education classes, and the funding shortfall meant they might have to assume up to 80% of the cost.[350]

The Office of Civil Rights became involved in the special education program in many school districts after it was discovered that a disproportionate number of black students were being placed into special education classes. New guidelines were handed down that required the districts to use an additional test to take into account cultural differences when evaluating students for placement in a special education program. The guidelines also required that a committee be formed to determine each student's eligibility for special education services. The committee would include the parent, a teacher, a principal, the district psychological examiner, and a member of the special education supervisory staff. The student could also attend if he or she wanted to do so. Parents could appeal decisions through the district administrative levels, the district Board of Education, and then the court system.[351]

The legislature raised state aid from $5.5 million to $12 million for the 1977-78 school year and to $14 million for 1978-79 school year.[352] This would still not be enough to get all Arkansas districts in compliance with the law by 1979. Although Arkansas was one of the first states to submit its 1977-78 plans for special education to the Office of Education, it was the only state to have its plans not be approved or to be disapproved. Commissioner Ford launched a letter-writing campaign, but it was to no avail. He even asked Governor David Pryor to make inquiries as to what was causing the delay. The major problem reportedly was that the timetable in the plan indicated that Arkansas would not be able to provide a full range of services to all of its approximately 45,000 students with disabilities by the deadline the federal government had set. The Office of Education was supposedly considering denying funding to the state for 1977-78 because it would not be complying with the federal law for the next year.[353]

This would be only a small bump in the road to providing special education services to students with disabilities. Today, the Arkansas Department of Education oversees a massive special education program. Districts now provide a variety of services, including not only resource rooms and self-contained classrooms but also "inclusion" classes in which special education students are placed into a regular academic classroom. In inclusion classes, a special education teacher assists the regular classroom teacher in providing individualized and differentiated instruction. Arch Ford's goal of providing equal educational opportunities to all Arkansas children had expanded to include those with disabilities.

Chapter 11: Public Kindergarten

Ed McCuistion, assistant commissioner for training services, began working at the state Department of Education in 1931. He had started advocating for public kindergarten in about 1949 and even drafted a bill that would permit districts to add these classes. The bill died in the legislature, but McCuistion—who was considered a pioneer in the kindergarten movement—kept track of developments in other states. In 1961, he began to campaign again for public kindergarten in Arkansas. By this time, there were about sixteen other states that had public kindergarten classes. McCuistion believed one of the biggest hurdles to providing kindergarten was getting more teachers trained for the elementary level; most prospective teachers were training to become secondary teachers instead. He likened education to a building—the elementary program had to provide a good foundation for students, and the foundation had to be sturdy or the upper floors would be weak.[354]

A Constitutional Issue

Ed McCuistion's boss, Arch Ford, was also beginning to see an increased demand by parents for kindergarten classes. Commissioner Ford said in a 1962 interview that young working mothers in industrialized areas were particularly interested in putting their children in kindergarten. He said that the main hindrance in providing public kindergarten was that the Arkansas Constitution only provided for the education of children ages six to twenty-one. A constitutional amendment would have to be approved by the legislature and voted on by the public before that could be changed. Just as with other issues, such as desegregation and special education, Ford believed that kindergarten programs should be designed by the local districts with the Department of Education playing an advisory role and providing financing.[355]

Two years later, Ford finally felt the legislature might be receptive to the idea of public kindergarten. He asked for a bill putting a constitutional amendment on the 1966 general election ballot. By this time, forty-three other states had permissive legislation that allowed their districts to provide kindergarten classes, while six states had mandatory kindergarten classes. In a 1964 interview, Governor Orval Faubus, who favored public kindergarten, also spoke out, saying that Arkansas was the only state in the union that did not have a kindergarten program of any kind.[356]

The legislature failed to pass the bill. The Senate passed the proposal, but became ensnared in a House filibuster a few minutes before the regular session ended. Ford was very upset. In a December 1966 interview, he expressed his frustration with a particular legislator, saying, "I understand that Representative Talbot Field of Hempstead County laughed as he filibustered and trapped the constitutional provision brought up in the House about six minutes before adjournment." He continued, "Well to me there is nothing laughable about closing the door to about 38,000 children each year." He said that the state should be in a position to afford these children kindergarten education to prepare them for modern educational demands.[357]

Commissioner Ford continued to push forward to provide public kindergarten. He asked Arkansas's attorney general, Bruce Bennett, for an opinion as to whether federal funding could be used by districts for kindergarten even if the state constitution did not allow the state to provide funding. Bennett said there was no prohibition in the constitution or state laws against spending federal money on children younger than six. In response, Ford released federal monies to districts that were conducting kindergarten classes for children who qualified under the Elementary and Secondary Education Act.[358]

Ford also continued to advocate publicly for the constitutional amendment and for public kindergarten. He explained in the December 1966 interview that, for many years, a large segment of educational experts believed that restricting education to a certain age group improved elementary and secondary education. "This was another fallacy and one which I opposed. I think the profession has come to realize that the more people involved in education the quicker the gains and improvements," he said. He pointed out that the constitutional restrictions are enforced for kindergarten, while the restrictions on adult education are ignored. Both restrictions should be removed, he argued.[359]

The state Department of Education had begun a pilot program for adult education in 1961 with little resistance. Local school boards applied for state aid to set up an experimental adult education program. A sum of $47,000 was allocated in the department budget that year for this program. Only state residents who were eighteen or older and who had failed to complete high school and had been out of school for six months or more were eligible to take the courses. Classes in language, mathematics, social studies, foreign languages, and science at the elementary and secondary level were taught. The state paid up to $3 an hour for each qualified teacher instructing these classes. The program was patterned after one that the federal government used after World War II to enable veterans to complete their high school education.[360]

In February 1967, Senator Joe T. Ford of Little Rock (who was Commissioner Ford's son) and Senator Clarence Bell of Parkin introduced a bill to amend the constitution so that kindergarten could be funded by the state. The senators argued that Arkansas was the only state that constitutionally prohibited public kindergarten. Amendment 53, as it would become known, would allow free education for persons over twenty-one and children under six. This time, the amendment proposal was passed by the legislature and was put on the ballot for the 1968 general election.[361]

Commissioner Ford spoke out in support of the kindergarten program at the Conway Rotary Club in November 1967. He explained that even though there were only seven states that had a developed kindergarten program, all states in the country except Arkansas had "permissive" legislation to allow the formation of the program. He said that voters would have a chance to change that by voting to remove the constitutional restrictions that limited the age of those who could be educated. He favored a program that would be "permissive" for those districts that wanted to develop a kindergarten program.[362] Amendment 53 would be approved by the voters in the general election of 1968, and Arkansas school districts could begin receiving state funding for public kindergartens.

A Statewide Kindergarten Program

Once the constitutional obstacle had been removed, funding would be the next obstacle that would keep the number of kindergartens from growing very rapidly. No appropriations were made in 1969. In 1970, however, the Department of Education asked for $4 million to fund kindergarten in the next biennium.[363] Instead, Governor Dale Bumpers asked for $500,000 for each year of the biennium.

That bill, however, was defeated in the Senate through a fluke of parliamentary procedure. At that time, the Senate had a policy that if a senator was going to be absent for a vote, he could "pair" with another senator who planned to vote just the opposite. When the roll call vote was taken, the "paired" senator was supposed to keep silent when his name was called. The pairs would be recorded after the roll call vote was finished. Senator Joe Ford had to be absent from the Senate the day the vote was taken for kindergarten funding, so he paired with a freshman senator, Senator Harold King of Sheridan. Unfortunately, when King's name was called, he mistakenly answered "nay." This caused the defeat of the kindergarten appropriations bill, as Lieutenant Governor Bob Riley, a stickler for parliamentary procedure, refused to allow Ford's vote of "aye" to be recorded.[364] Proponents managed to get the bill brought for reconsideration the next day, but it was again defeated by one vote when a senator who voted for it earlier changed his vote.[365]

The legislature appropriated $200,000 in 1972 for a pilot kindergarten program. Most of the money was used to train teachers. In 1973, Governor Bumpers asked the Legislative Council to appropriate funding for a statewide kindergarten program. He proposed that the state help pay for public kindergarten in any school district that wanted to establish a program. He recommended $4,362,242 for kindergartens in the 1973-74 school year and $5,761,206 for 1974-75. The Legislative Council denied his request.[366] Instead, they recommended $250,000 for each year of the next biennium, saying the program was too expensive and would only benefit rich school districts. Representative John E. Miller of Melbourne also proposed adding $15,380,000 to the governor's recommendations to pay for construction of kindergarten buildings in the districts. He said the poorer districts did not have the money to build classrooms and therefore would not be able to take advantage of state aid for kindergarten. His proposal was defeated by the Legislative Council as well.[367]

Bumpers would not give up the fight. He said he intended to pursue his budget request "very vigorously" in the legislative session. He said the expansion of the kindergarten program had a "very high" priority in his administration and, if anything, his proposal was too modest. In response to the criticism about it benefiting only rich districts, the governor said he had put in safeguards to make sure that all districts had an equal chance at obtaining state aid.[368] He even told reporters that it was so important he would rather do away with twelfth grade than have no kindergarten program.[369]

Bumpers's kindergarten bill was introduced into the Senate by three senators: Joe T. Ford of Little Rock, Clarence Bell of Parkin, and Jim Caldwell of Rogers. The bill would provide free kindergarten, with 20,000 children being served in the second year. At first, it looked as if the bill would not get out of the Senate Education Committee, but two senators ended up changing their votes and giving it a "do pass" to be sent to the full Senate. Senator Joe T. Ford was one of five senators on the committee who gave the bill a "do pass." The full Senate passed the bill and sent it to the House, which also passed the bill 52 to 21. The bill did not provide appropriations, but a later bill was passed to appropriate funds.[370]

Betty Bumpers, Arch Ford, Ruby Ford, and Governor Dale Bumpers in 1974. *Photo courtesy of Joe T. Ford*

Commissioner Ford estimated that only about one-third of the school districts would be ready to start kindergarten programs in the next two years. In order to receive state funding, a school district would have to show that could it provide adequate space in its own buildings. It would also have to provide qualified teachers and meet the minimum program standards that were set by the state.[371] This was why some senators were concerned that the program would be implemented only in districts that could afford to meet those requirements.[372]

It was estimated that the program would eventually cost $11 or $12 million to fund classes in all districts. The Department of Education planned to fund kindergartens at $9,000 per classroom. Commissioner Ford told the Senate Education Committee at the hearings that there were 365 teachers who had been trained to teach kindergarten. Their training had been financed by an earlier $200,000 appropriation for a pilot program. He pointed out that if the state did not fund a statewide kindergarten program, it would have instead trained kindergarten teachers for other states.[373]

When Bumpers signed the bill, which became Act 83 of 1973, he said he might have to ask for more money than he had originally requested for the next biennium. He said it would depend on "how we come out with the education budgets and some other budgets and the results of a survey the Department is conducting to determine how many districts would participate in the kindergarten program initially." It had just been announced that President Richard Nixon was dismantling the federal Head Start program, so that would end up affecting the demand for kindergarten classes.[374] The legislature eventually appropriated $5.5 million for 1973-74 and $6.5 million for 1974-75.[375]

Keeping Up with Demand for Kindergarten Classes

Nearly half of all kindergarten-aged children were in school for the 1973-74 school year. There probably would have been even more classes, but some districts could not provide a teacher certified in early childhood education to teach the class. The urban areas had less trouble finding qualified teachers thanks to the pilot training programs begun by Governor Winthrop Rockefeller.[376]

In August 1974, Commissioner Ford reported that about $1 million of the funding was not used because soaring building costs in the past year had made it impossible for the districts to get classroom space ready for the new kindergarten classes. On a positive note, however, he said that the state colleges and universities had accelerated their efforts to train early childhood teachers and there would be plenty of trained teachers to meet the demand if they could just get the classrooms built.[377]

Anticipating a big increase in district applications for kindergarten funding, the governor asked the legislature for $11 million for fiscal year 1975. It was granted. About 44% of the 34,000 five-year-olds in the state attended kindergarten in 1973-74, and the Department expected 60 to 65% to attend in the 1974-75 school year. Arch Ford commented at the time, "It isn't because of lack of demand in most of the districts. The program is popular and school officials are under considerable pressure from parents to offer programs." He said that, in the past year, districts had offered 444 full-day units. In the current year, there were 654 full-day units. The half-day programs grew from 273 to 293. In a special session, the legislature raised aid for a full-day program from $9,000 to $9,500 per class and $4,500 to $4,750 per half-day class. Many districts had a half-day program because they did not have enough certified teachers and had one teacher teaching two classes.[378]

Commissioner Ford reported in the Department of Education newsletter in July 1976 that more than 80% of all eligible five-year-olds were enrolled for kindergarten in the 1976-77 school year, but the kindergarten classes were still suffering from a lack of funding. The legislature gave districts enough aid to give the kindergarten teachers a $600 raise, but the districts did not get enough funding to start new classes for the 2,000 more students who wanted to be educated.[379] Later that year, Governor David Pryor got a bill passed that raised kindergarten funding by $612,000 for 1977-78 and by $1,412,420 for 1978-79.[380]

Although Arch Ford was a major advocate of making it mandatory for Arkansas five-year-olds to attend kindergarten, he would not live to see that happen. Today, Arkansas is one of twelve states that require districts to offer a full-day kindergarten program. Thirty-four states require their districts to have a half-day kindergarten program. There are sixteen states, including Arkansas, that have mandatory kindergarten attendance.[381] Arkansas also specifies that

Governor David Pryor signing a bill to raise kindergarten funding. *Photo courtesy of Arch Ford Collection, UA Special Collections*

kindergarteners must attend six hours a day, or 1,080 hours per year. All children who turn five on or before August 1 must attend, although parents can sign a waiver for a child to delay kindergarten for a year if the child will not be six before August 1 of that school year. In addition, the Arkansas School Readiness Committee has written a list of thirty-eight indicators for parents to use to make sure that their child is ready for kindergarten. Common Core Standards have also been written for kindergarten.

Chapter 12: Textbooks and Fire Protection

Although the state of Arkansas had been furnishing textbooks to grades one through eight since 1936, it did not provide any funding for high school textbooks. There had been efforts made at various times, but the Arkansas Education Association usually opposed the idea because the money would be taken out of the Public School Fund, which provided salaries to teachers. Another struggle faced by early Arkansas schools was providing fire protection for the schools it had invested in so much.

Free Textbooks for High Schools

In the summer of 1952, State Representative Roy H. Gaylean asked the Legislative Council to do a study on the feasibility of providing free high school textbooks. The study showed that most states had a free textbook program, although the programs varied in terms of how many grades received the free textbooks. The initial cost of purchasing high school textbooks at that time was estimated to be about $2 million, with about $400,000 needed each year for replacement costs. The legislature did not take any action, however, because of the pressure to increase teachers' salaries.[382] In 1959, State Representative Chadd L. Durrett of Union County introduced a bill for free textbooks in the high school, but the House of Representatives turned it down 42 to 29.[383]

In 1962, Representative Gaylean of Benton County again asked the Legislative Council to investigate whether the state could expand its free textbook program to cover the cost of high school textbooks. H. T. Steele, the director of instructional materials for the state Department of Education, reported at that time that the average cost of providing textbooks was about $2.93 per grade-school pupil. The legislature had budgeted about $1 million for textbooks for the 1961–62 school year, but the state Board of Education had cut that figure to $940,000 because of low revenue collection. It was pointed out by other education officials that Mississippi, Oklahoma, Texas, Louisiana, Georgia, Florida, and New Mexico—all in the southern part of the country—were among the states already providing free textbooks in grades one through twelve.[384]

Nothing was done in 1962, and the issue did not come up again until 1965. In October 1965, Commissioner Arch Ford told the Legislative Council that he had received more complaints from parents about the cost of high school textbooks than about any other subject. He suggested that the state either provide the books or purchase the books at bulk rates and sell them to the students at cost. The Department of Education had estimated the initial cost of the free-textbook program to be $3 million, with the annual replacement cost being $750,000. At that time, the budget for textbooks in grades one through eight was $1,050,000, which was up $50,000 from the previous year.[385]

Senator Clarence Bell of Parkin, a former school superintendent, asked the Legislative Council to undertake a study to determine the feasibility and cost of extending the free-textbook program to the high school level. He suggested that such a study should include a determination of whether there was federal money available to assist in paying for the textbooks. He said, "There isn't any question that the cost of high school textbooks is high. I think that the state, through competitive bids, could command a far better price on a volume basis." The council agreed to conduct the study and submit recommendations to the 1967 General Assembly.[386]

Jim Johnson, the Democratic nominee for governor in 1966, advocated using the $2.7 million accumulation in the Public School Fund for expanding free textbooks into the high schools. Arch Ford commented at the time that he was pleased that Johnson would take a stand on expanding free textbooks and hoped Republican gubernatorial candidate Winthrop Rockefeller would also recommend the expansion. The Arkansas Education Association (AEA) tried to make sure the money went to teachers' salaries. It asked Faubus to call a special session of the legislature before the election and put the $2.7 million in teachers' salaries. Governor Faubus, however, did not commit himself to a special session in the weeks before the election.[387]

In an October 1966 press conference, Commissioner Ford again promoted the idea of providing free textbooks at the high school level. He said, "Governor Faubus is leaving the state in such a fine economic position that it no longer is an either-or proposition. The state can do both." Faubus publicly agreed with Ford. He said Ford had conferred with him on the shape of the state's economy and that it was good. Faubus said it was so good, in fact, that the state might end up having a much larger general fund surplus than the $21 million he had mentioned a few weeks earlier. Winthrop Rockefeller, the Republican gubernatorial nominee, called a press conference later that morning to state his positions on education.[388]

The Education Committee of the Legislative Council met the day after Ford's press conference and announced that it would recommend that the state provide free textbooks to high schools but only if enough money was available. The committee's study found that the cost in the first year would be about $3 million based on an estimate of $25 per pupil; it would cost about $7 per pupil the next year to maintain the program. The cost estimates provided by the Department of Education were based on providing books in the sixteen basic high school units.

One concern was that some districts were currently receiving federal assistance for free textbooks for students of parents who earned less than $2,000 a year. William H. Moore, Arkansas Director of ESEA, had notified the committee that federal matching funds could not be used if the state adopted a free-textbook plan for all high school students. Arch Ford told the committee that the districts would then be able to use that money somewhere else. One of the legislators on the committee, Senator Bob Douglas of Texarkana, made the point that there were many other students who were being deprived. He said students in large families in which the income was more than $2,000 were often under greater hardships than students in small families that made less than $2,000.[389]

Senator Douglas introduced the bill for extending the free-textbook program to high schools. Although it did not sail through the legislature because of the demands for increasing teacher salaries, it was finally passed as Act 334 of 1967. Governor Winthrop Rockefeller signed it into law in March 1967. Unfortunately, the act did not specify *when* the state was to expand the textbook program, and an amendment had been attached to the bill barring the expansion until teachers' salaries reached 80% of the national average. Even so, proponents of the free-textbook program considered this a victory because the state was now officially on record as committing to providing free textbooks for high schools.[390]

Six years later, however, the high schools still did not have free textbooks. Governor Dale Bumpers called it a major priority for the 1973 legislative session. The Department of Education asked the Board of Education to submit a request for an initial $5.3 million and about $1 million a year to run the program into the 1973–74 biennium budget. The board rejected the recommendation, but Governor Bumpers took up the cause and said he planned to use surplus funds to pay for extending the free-textbook program into the high schools. The department had told him that an "unbelievable number" of pupils had to share books with other students. Bumpers said that a minimal requirement for a good education system included free textbooks for all students. He argued that the initial cost of $5.3 million spread over two or three years would be the greatest investment required, but the program would cost only about $1 million a year after the initial outlay.[391]

A bill was introduced into the legislature in 1973 to begin providing the free high school textbooks in the fall of 1973. Bumpers's original request was reduced to $6 million, with $5 million for the initial costs and $1 million more to be appropriated if the money was available. Districts would be authorized to buy books on one basic subject each year for six years. The books would be district property, and the district could buy used books if they were on the state's approved list of textbooks.[392]

Commissioner Ford named a group of eighty-one teachers to serve on nine new committees for high school textbook selection. He also told the Board of Education that although the law did not require it, he had made sure the racial makeup of each committee approximated the racial makeup of the state as a whole; on most of the committees, two of the nine members were black. The committees would choose texts for English, science, mathematics, social studies, practical arts, health and physical education, fine arts, and special education. Dean H. Whiteside, coordinator of instructional materials for the Department of Education, recommended a method of reimbursing local districts for textbooks on receipt of the district's canceled invoices. He also recommended that Arch Ford be empowered to "make whatever rules and regulations we deem necessary" concerning the distribution of the books until the board's next meeting in June. (At that time, the Board of Education was only meeting bi-monthly.)[393]

So persistence finally paid off, and free textbooks were made available for the high school students in Arkansas. In addition to his role in getting the legislation passed to provide for the free textbooks, Commissioner Ford also was responsible for setting up the first procedures for purchasing and distributing those textbooks to districts.

Fire Marshal Program

One of the greatest problems in early Arkansas schools was the loss of school buildings due to fire. During Arch Ford's early years as commissioner of education, the legislature passed Act 61 of 1959, which inaugurated a safety program aimed at eliminating school fires. A Junior Fire Marshal program, in which only about 80% of the schools were participating at the time, was mandated in all the schools of Arkansas. The program named students to act as fire monitors for their schools to raise awareness and eliminate potential fire hazards. The program also called for fire safety inspections and regular fire drills. The program was in its eleventh year in Arkansas when the legislature decided to require all districts to participate in the program. The program had been credited with reducing school fires dramatically. Before the Junior Fire Marshal program had been enacted throughout the state, there were some twenty-five major school fires each year.[394]

Two years after the implementation of Act 61 of 1959, state Department of Education officials reported that the fire marshal program had almost completely eliminated major school fires. The number of fires in Arkansas's schools had been reduced by about 90% from a decade earlier.[395]

Chapter 13: The Ford Family Legacy Continues

In April 2015, Economics Arkansas (formerly the Arkansas Council on Economic Education) honored the Ford family for its dedication to economic education and its contributions to the economy of Arkansas. While Arch Ford is considered the "father" of Arkansas economic education, his son, Joe, and his grandson, Scott, have also made and continue to make significant contributions to the economy of Arkansas, the nation, and the world through their leadership at Alltel and Westrock Coffee.

Legacy of Father to Son

Joe Ford was raised in a loving household by both his parents. Arch Ford did not believe in corporal punishment for his son. In an era in which that type of punishment was implemented with regularity, Arch believed that "the greatest power, the greatest force in the world is—love. And love—not fear—is the answer."[396] Joe was also raised in a home where his parents made sure he was in church every Sunday.

Arch, Joe, and Ruby Ford in 1942.
Photo courtesy of Joe T. Ford

After Joe graduated from Conway High School in 1955, he attended Arkansas State College (now Arkansas State University—ASU) in Jonesboro before transferring to the University of Arkansas (UA) in Fayetteville. There, he majored in business and minored in economics. After he graduated from UA in 1959, he married Jo Ellen Wilbourn of Conway. They were married at First Baptist Church by the Reverend James H. Street, who became pastor of the church in 1954 and served until 1961. Arch served as his son's best man. Their reception was held at the home of Jo Ellen's parents, Mr. and Mrs. Hugh Wilbourn Jr.

Young men at that time had to go through basic training, so Joe spent some time in the army after graduation. He then served as a captain and unit commander in the Arkansas National Guard. After his military service, Joe went to work for Allied Telephone Company selling advertisements for the Yellow Pages section of its telephone book. The company was owned by Hugh Wilbourn Jr. (Joe's father-in-law) and Charles Miller. Hugh's sister, Marion, was married to Charles Miller, and both Wilbourn and Miller had worked together at Southwestern Bell before going into business together in 1943 to form what would eventually be Allied Telephone.

Joe Ford with his father, Arch Ford, in the Arkansas State Senate in 1981. *Photo courtesy of Joe T. Ford*

In 1983, on the heels of the breakup of AT&T, Allied Telephone merged its operations with that of Mid-Continent, a telephone company based in Ohio. The new company was named Alltel. Joe Ford became the president and chief operating officer of Alltel[397] and assumed the role of chief executive officer in 1987. In 1991, he became chairman of the board. He would lead Alltel to become a major telecommunications provider.

Joe described his father as a loving person. Joe said of his father, "He loved education. He was the first in his family to get a college degree. Money meant nothing as compared to education for him personally. He wanted good people involved in that work. He was a wonderful person with a great sense of humor. We talked often."[398]

The values that his father instilled in him would contribute to the success Joe Ford had in business. He valued his employees and believed in getting the right people in the right place and then allowing them to make good decisions and do good work.[399] He said in one interview, "I look at business as a people-to-people thing—honesty, integrity, and respect—and I do business on that basis." He believed that good employees and customer service were the keys to the success that Alltel had in the 1980s and 1990s.[400] His impact on the success of Alltel was tremendous. Throughout the corporation, he was recognized for his values and his strong ethical standards.

Joe Ford had a high level of compassion for his employees. Dennis Foster, vice chairman of Alltel, said, "He knows people. He remembers people." Mike Flynn, a group president for Alltel who would eventually become president of Alltel's communications operations, said, "Joe is very consistent about his values, and that's communicated constantly." Jerry Fetzer, vice president of shared services, said, "Joe Ford has created a culture that says we're going to work hard, we're going to be aggressive, but we're going to do it with ethics and integrity."[401]

In 2000, Joe Ford's individual efforts in growing Allied and helping it become a major telecommunications company were recognized by the United States Telecom Association (USTA). The organization awarded him its highest honor, the Distinguished Service Medallion, in recognition of his "outstanding contributions to advance the telecommunications industry and USTA."[402]

Joe T. Ford as State Senator

Joe Ford inherited his father's enthusiasm for public service and he ran in 1966 for a position in the Arkansas State Senate representing Pulaski and Lonoke Counties. He said, "My father was always encouraging and supportive. I went to him when I was thinking about running for the Senate. He said it's your decision. He never tried to push me one way or another."[403] Ford defeated three other candidates in the 1966 election.

As a state senator, he championed many of his father's educational reforms. He helped get legislation passed for public school kindergartens, free high school textbooks, equal education for children with disabilities, modernization of school facilities, vocational-technical education, and major salary raises for teachers—in addition to the significantly higher taxes to pay for these programs.[404] He also helped with the merger of Little Rock University into the University of Arkansas system in 1969 to become the University of Arkansas at Little Rock.[405]

In 1977, Joe Ford was recognized by the Arkansas Education Association (AEA) for being the only state senator who did not vote against positions taken by the organization in the recent legislative session. AEA had supported fifteen different bills ranging from public school employees' insurance to a teachers' job security bill.[406]

There was talk of Joe Ford running for governor, but he withdrew from politics in 1982 to focus on developing Alltel. That decision would result in the development of one of the largest telecommunications companies in the nation. Joe retired from his position as CEO in July 2002 and passed the day-to-day leadership to his son, Scott Ford.

Scott Ford

The Ford family legacy of Christian values and public service would pass down through Joe Ford to Arch's grandson, Scott Ford. Scott graduated from the University of Arkansas in 1984 with a degree in finance. He then went to work for Merrill Lynch financial company before being hired as an assistant in the corporate finance division of Stephens Inc., the Little Rock investment firm owned by Jackson and Witt Stephens. He put together billion-dollar deals for Stephens for ten years until he went to work at Alltel in 1996.

When Scott Ford was twelve, he had a conversation with his father about the career he would pursue after school. His father, Joe Ford, told him he would support him in whatever he chose to do, but he said that he did not want them to ever work together. Joe remembered the pressure of having to work for a family member and did not want his son to have to feel that same pressure. Even when it became evident that someone with Scott's energy and enthusiasm was needed at Alltel, Joe was reluctant to bring him aboard because of "too much family."[407]

Finally, in January 1996, Joe asked Scott to come to Alltel as executive vice president. The Telecommunications Act of 1996, which opened up local telephone markets to competition, had thrown the whole industry into upheaval, and he needed Scott to help him work through the changes. Scott was given the responsibility for the company's communications businesses and corporate staff functions. In 1997, he would succeed his father as president. He would take over the duties of chief operating officer in 1998.

Before Joe retired, both he and Scott would spend a lot of time encouraging the employees of the various services to communicate with each other. When the company was smaller, Joe had spent a lot of time walking the hallways of the business, talking to people and shaking hands. But as the business grew larger, he had tried to give them room to work and not feel that he was looking over their shoulder. Scott encouraged him to go back to his old habit and help him work on improving the corporate culture.[408]

Scott became CEO of Alltel when Joe retired in 2002. He would continue to grow the company. In August 2002, Alltel added more than 700,000 customers when it acquired CenturyTel's wireless properties. This gave Alltel 7.5 million customers in twenty-six states. It also acquired 600,000 access lines in Kentucky from Verizon.[409] In 2005, Alltel announced it would become a wireless-only company and spun off its wireline business and merged it with Valor Telecom to form Windstream Communications. In May 2007, Scott Ford led Alltel through its $27.5 billion sale to two private entities, TPG (Texas

Pacific Group) Capital and GS (Goldman Sachs) Capital Partners. Verizon would acquire the company from these private investors in 2008, making Verizon the largest cell phone provider in the nation.[410]

Rwanda and Westrock Coffee

About three years before the Alltel buyout, Scott Ford had been in Rwanda helping develop Sonrise School, a school that blended local children and orphans to help provide a better education for orphans. He found himself in an after-dinner conversation with President Paul Kagame. Kagame led Rwanda out of the 1994 genocide that had occurred in that country and was at that time trying to help his country enter an era of economic growth. As the two men discussed how Western imperialism had handicapped the entrepreneurial spirit of the African people, they began talking about the three basic freedoms—spiritual, political, and economic—that had caused Western civilization to prosper over the last 2,500 years. They talked about how important it was to have all three of these if growth was to occur. Both agreed that real economic growth could be achieved through a strong capitalistic economy rather than through outside charity.[411]

Scott got involved with the "Friends of Rwanda" network, a small circle of U.S. businesspeople who wanted to help with Rwanda's development. He began assisting the Rwandan government, reviewing contracts with Western companies and working on ways to expand Rwanda's power grid. He also participated in Kagame's Presidential Advisory Council. He eventually decided that the best way he could help Rwanda was to directly invest in its economy by starting a private company that he could use to bring about social change and demonstrate the impact of economic profitability. His grandfather's legacy about the importance of economic education was about to hit the ground in Rwanda.

In 2009, after the Alltel buyout was finalized, Scott took a team to Rwanda to explore the possibility of opening a coffee export company, Rwanda Trading Company. The coffee industry in Rwanda was significant, and coffee is the second-largest marketed commodity in the world. Rwandan coffee had, in the last several years, become one of the highest-quality coffees in the world, thanks to Kagame's policies. He removed trade barriers, created incentives to invest in coffee production, and encouraged small-scale coffee entrepreneurs.

Scott decided that starting Rwanda Trading Company would also help him in achieving his social goals as well. More than 500,000 farmers produced Rwandan coffee, and creating a business that would buy the coffee would help all of those people and their families. He could also model how a business relationship with African entrepreneurs and foreign investors could be beneficial for both parties.

Scott looked at other African countries, but in the end chose Rwanda because of its legal system. One of the things that must be present for capitalism to be successful is a law code that protects business and private property. Scott said, "Rwanda has a set of laws that they enforce, and if they come against a problem, they fix it. When Rwanda shows that it's actually attracting capital by being honest, then others will start saying, 'Maybe we ought to try that approach.'"[412]

Back in Little Rock, Scott and his father, Joe, bought and renovated a 56,000-square-foot roasting facility so they could roast the beans they bought from the Rwandan farmers. They helped the farmers make capital improvements in their washing stations and even gave them low-rate loans during the dry season. His Rwandan managers were trained in supply-chain management as well as financial analysis so that the whole process could be as productive as possible from field to factory.

Scott had spent weekends with his grandfather while growing up. As Arch Ford began to have health problems in his retirement years,

Scott was determined to spend more time with him. He wanted to gather all the wisdom that he could. In a 2015 interview, Scott Ford recalled a health scare that his grandfather had in the early 1980s. He remembers sitting with his grandfather during this time and asking him what he thought was the most important thing to mark a man's life. His grandfather replied, "Perseverance. Many people who would have been successful quit." Later, when he was thinking about the heavy burden and the high risk of doing business in Rwanda, he thought about quitting and remembered what his grandfather said about perseverance.[413]

Not only has Westrock become a sustainable model for economic development in Africa, it has also become a way to show Rwandans the benefits of free enterprise and capitalism. It has provided them with a cash income, which has helped lower infant mortality rates and made education possible for the next generation. And, as Arch Ford had instilled in his son and grandson, education is the key to a better life. In a 2015 interview, Joe Ford said, "Scott is continuing his grandfather's idea of education in this respect...the children of Rwanda get a better opportunity."[414]

Chapter 14: Other Legacies of Arch Ford

One of the constants in Arch Ford's life was his dedication to his faith. He had been raised in a Christian home and had inherited a legacy of leadership in the church from the Ford family as well as the Clements family. His grandfather, George Washington Ford, was a minister and brought his family to Arkansas to pastor a church in Plumerville. He then moved to Faulkner County and pastored Pleasant Valley Baptist Church before becoming the first pastor of Bethlehem Baptist Church in northern Faulkner County.

His maternal uncles helped establish the Bethlehem Baptist Church, located about three miles north of Wooster. "Every Sunday morning without fail they loaded their families into hacks or wagons and drove on a dirt road two to three miles north to Bethlehem Baptist Church," said Justin Williams Sr. "After the service, and on those Sundays devoted to 'all-day singing and dinner on the ground,' they discussed crops and politics with their friends."[415]

In an interview shortly after he became commissioner of education, Arch Ford talked about the fact that four of his uncles were Baptist preachers. They did not belong to the same clan of Baptists, however, so family reunions were always enlivened by spirited debates. "I didn't know enough about

Arch and Ruby Ford celebrated their 50th anniversary in 1977. *Photo courtesy of Joe T. Ford*

the Bible to judge whether or not these arguments were worthwhile," said Arch, "but I noticed they could all eat fried chicken and that they agreed on one point—they socked their converts under the water. They believed too in the doctrine—'once saved, always saved.' That was about the most comforting thing I had heard."[416]

While his maternal uncles were charter members of Bethlehem Baptist, his family helped organize the First Baptist Church at Wooster. Arch was raised to serve in his church. Wherever he lived, he became involved in his church and served faithfully.

Arch Ford's Christian Leadership

Arch was a deacon and Sunday school superintendent at First Baptist Church during the time he was living in Conway. He raised his son Joe there, and the family never missed Sunday services. When Arch Ford was interviewed shortly after he became commissioner, reporter Fay Williams made note of the facts that Arch was a tither, Mrs. Ford was a first-grade Sunday school teacher, and Joe had not missed Sunday school in the past three years.[417] In Proverbs 22:6 it says, "Train up a child in the way he should go; even when he is old he will not depart from it." One of Arch Ford's biggest legacies was in fulfilling that verse. As an adult, Joe continued his dedication to his faith and served as a deacon in his church, Pulaski Heights Baptist Church.

Security Savings and Loan

Arch Ford was also part of a group of Conway businessmen who organized Security Savings and Loan in March 1960. It became the fifth savings and loan in Arkansas to operate as a stock company. Its primary purpose was to encourage industry, thrift, homebuilding, and savings within a fifty-mile radius of Conway. There were initially forty stockholders. The board of directors included George G. Shaw Sr., president; Dr. Edwin L. Dunaway, vice president; Hugh R. Wilbourn Jr., secretary-treasurer; Lillard L. Bolls; and Arch W. Ford. Robert E.

Sly was chosen to be the first manager.

Security's charter was issued by the Arkansas Banking Department in 1960. The company was approved by the Federal Home Loan Bank in Little Rock and the Federal Savings and Loan Insurance Corporation. The savings and loan started with initial assets of $187,500 but within a month of opening for business had increased assets to $338,343. Assets by December 31, 1965, were $4,575,081.[418]

The bank opened for business July 1, 1961, and was originally located at 1000 Front Street in the Shaw Building. It had two receiving windows. In 1967, the bank built a new office at 1122 Van Ronkle.[419] This new building was constructed out of pre-cast stone. The $122,900 building was erected by Richardson Construction of Little Rock.

Arch Ford remained on the board of directors along with David L. Baker, Lillard L. Bolls, Marvin Cantrell, Dr. Ed Dunaway, George G. Shaw Jr., Robert E. Sly, S. T. Smith, and Hugh R. Wilbourn Jr.[420] Ford served as chairman of the board and even took over as president when Ed Dunaway passed away in April 1975. Ed Dunaway and his wife were the largest stockholders in the bank at that time.[421] Bill Johnson would take over as president in December 1977, but Arch Ford remained as chairman of the board.[422]

Masonic Lodge

Arch Ford was a member of the East Fork Masonic Lodge #327 in Wooster for over fifty years. The lodge was established in 1874 after the Green Grove Lodge moved to Conway. Lodge members met in a former Methodist Episcopal Church building until the present lodge building was constructed in 1941 on the same site.

Central Baptist College Building Fund Drive

In 1968–69, Central Baptist College in Conway held a fundraising campaign to finish a new building that would house the J. E. Cobb Library as well as the school's administrative offices. Money was also raised for a new men's dorm. Plans also included remodeling for existing dorms and the building of new parking lots to serve the campus. Arch Ford was selected to head the fundraising campaign.[423]

Father of the Year

In 1971, Arch Ford was named "Father of the Year" by *Arkansas Baptist Newsmagazine*. His son, Joe, nominated him and included the following in his letter of recommendation: "Dad has not only given me good advice, but he has always demonstrated by his actions the highest of ideals. He has always been active in the church and expected the same from his family. He has shown the ability to go to the heart of a problem and not be delayed by the trivial. He has taught me that honesty, fairness, integrity, and hard work are the keystones to success and he has always tried to live up to his own expectations."[424]

By this time, Arch and Ruby Ford had moved to Horseshoe Mountain in northern Faulkner County and were members of Greenbrier First Baptist Church. Ford taught the men's Bible class and had been a deacon there for many years. The award was presented to him at the church on Father's Day. Rev. Erwin L. McDonald, editor of *Arkansas Baptist*, presented the award.[425]

The Fords later moved their membership to Bethlehem Baptist Church, where Ford's grandfather had been the first pastor and his maternal uncles had been charter members. He became a deacon there and taught the men's Bible class. Ruby Ford helped organize the vacation Bible school.

Gideon Dignitary Bible

In 1978, Arch Ford was honored by the Conway Camp of Gideons International with a Gideon Dignitary Bible. The honor is bestowed annually by the Gideons to outstanding individuals. Gideons International is an association of Christian business professionals and their families who tell people about Jesus through sharing personally and providing Bibles and New Testaments. They often give out New

Testaments in colleges, prisons and jails, and hospitals and medical offices. They also place Bibles in hotel rooms. Dr. Audie Lynch, longtime educator, presented to the award to Ford before a crowd of about 200 at the Pastor's Appreciation Banquet at the Holiday Inn in Conway.

Rev. R. B. Hoshaw, Ford's pastor at Bethlehem Baptist Church, said this about the award: "Not only is Dr. Ford an outstanding educator but he is also a dedicated Christian family man and church man. He is a faithful deacon in the Bethlehem Church and he is the highly respected teacher of the men's Bible class there. He is a member of the Advisory Committee for the Central Baptist College Building Fund Drive in Conway. As his pastor I rejoice in this recognition of him as a fine Christian man and an outstanding public servant. I applaud this action by the Gideons of the Conway Camp."[426]

Arkansas State Teachers College Alumni

Arch served as president of the Alumni Association for Arkansas State Teachers College (ASTC) in 1963.[427] The University of Central Arkansas, as ASTC would eventually be renamed, would honor Arch Ford as a Distinguished Alumni in 1992. The posthumous award included a profile that said, "Mr. Ford's stamp on public education in Arkansas has been widely acclaimed as exceptional and enduring." It also said that he was "one of the most influential men in education in the history of the State of Arkansas." Ford's bronze portrait hangs in the Buffalo Alumni Hall at the university.[428]

Imparting Wisdom through Speeches

Arch Ford gave hundreds of speeches during the years he was commissioner and even some speeches after he retired. The following speech, given to faculty members at Newport Special School District on August 29, 1973, was particularly interesting, as it was addressed to teachers. In the speech, titled "Put Your Ego in Your Pocket," he discussed a teacher's ego: "Ego is the source of eternal individuality.

It causes a person to think or act with the perspective that one's self is the center, the object, and the norm of all experience. It is ego that makes you believe that you are the most important person in the world to you." He told the story of four teachers who influenced his life. Each controlled his ego and encouraged him to do the very best job he could. He concluded, "A Master Teacher knows that even though ego is one of his primary assets, only when he puts his ego in his pocket can he tolerate in others what he tolerates in himself."[429]

Chapter 15: The Retirement Years

E arly in 1978, Arch Ford told Governor David Pryor that he intended to retire as commissioner of education sometime during the year. Pryor was running for the U.S. Senate, so he would not be seeking another term as governor. Attorney General Bill Clinton would instead be seeking the Democratic nomination for governor. Clinton was elected as the Democratic gubernatorial candidate in the primary, and, at that time in Arkansas, Democrats were sure to become governor. In August, Ford told Clinton that he planned to retire before Clinton took office.

Ford notified the Board of Education and Governor Pryor formally in September that he would retire December 1. He said he wanted to give the board enough formal notice so that it would have adequate time to search for a new commissioner. He also wanted to give his successor a chance to recommend his or her own budget priorities to the new governor before the 1979 legislative session.[430]

Governor Pryor proclaimed December 1 as "Arch Ford Appreciation Day" in honor of his many years of educational service. The Department of Education announced that there would be a program at 10:30 a.m. that day at the Arch Ford Education Complex on the State Capitol Mall. Representatives from the department's various boards and commissions would speak, and the associate directors would make presentations. There would be an afternoon reception for invited guests, including members of the governor's cabinet, state legislators, and school administrators, as well as retirees from the Department of Education and the teaching profession.[431] There would also be a tribute to Arch Ford on AETN.[432]

The Joint Interim Committee on Education for the General Assembly honored Commissioner Ford by issuing Joint Resolution 77-76. The resolution said he had displayed "unusual knowledge and foresight in education matters" and had worked "tirelessly to improve education in Arkansas." It also said that under his wise direction, "public education in Arkansas has improved significantly and has been expanded to include public kindergarten, vocational-technical education, and equal educational opportunities for the disabled." It said that Ford's retirement would be a "great loss to the people of Arkansas and his guidance and direction in education will truly be missed."[433]

The Arkansas Council on Economic Education commissioned a portrait of Arch Ford to be hung in the lobby of the Education Building. Little Rock artist Betty Dortch Russell, who would later marry former governor Sid McMath, was commissioned to paint it. The painting was presented on December 1 on "behalf of friends and admirers whose private contributions made possible the tribute to his long and distinguished career as Chief State School Officer of Arkansas."[434]

This portrait of Arch Ford, painted by Betty Dortch Russell, was commissioned by the Arkansas Council on Economic Education to honor him for his years of service as the chief state school officer of Arkansas. The portrait was presented on Arch Ford Appreciation Day, December 1, 1978, and still hangs in the lobby of the Arch Ford Education Building on the Arkansas State Capitol grounds in Little Rock. *Photo courtesy of Ron Beckman*

One of the gifts the Department of Education staff presented to him on Arch Ford Day was his office desk and chair. Dorothy Gillam, his administrative assistant, said "he loved the desk and chair in his office" and "he was beside himself" when they presented this gift to him. The auditorium was filled with people. She said there were "a lot of sad employees. Several left the agency when he retired." She was not happy that he was retiring, but she understood. She was "pleased he wanted to do some things with his family, enjoy his home, farm, even when there was a storm in the area, enjoy running down stairs to cover up from the storm."[435]

Bessie Moore was one of the speakers in the Arch Ford Day program. She said:

> Not one time in my long career in the Department of Education did I ever go to Mr. Ford when I was discouraged or uncertain about something that he did not find time to sit down and help me work through the perplexity. All of us have had that experience. Always a supporter and friend, his door is open to everyone. He is equally concerned with achievements or failures. He has a knack for helping you analyze your failures and profit from them. The thing that probably endears him most to his fellow workers is that he has feeling for you as well as the job you are doing. In a recent conversation with me he said "People—that's what life is all about" and he behaved accordingly.
>
> Dr. Ford's appearance on TV talk programs has been a matter of conscience. He felt that the people have a right to understand education issues that are of concern to them, and where the Department Director stands on these issues. Many times he has been able to allay their fears and sometimes to spur them to action.
>
> There is no doubt that his influence made the difference in securing adoption of both kindergarten and community college programs. In each case, it was necessary to change the Constitution, no mean feat, to allow the state to spend money on children under six for kindergartens and on adults over 21 for community colleges.
>
> The vibrant quality of Dr. Ford's service in the field of education in Arkansas leaves an imprint that will live on. Thousands who may never know him personally will profit from his leadership, his statesmanship and his vision.[436]

Ford was also honored at the department's eighteenth-annual Christmas dinner on December 10, 1979, at the Little Rock Camelot Inn. The dinner was attended by about 450 people. Governor-elect Bill Clinton spoke, saying that he hoped Ford would be pleased "with the degree with which he and I agree about the direction and needs of public schools and education in Arkansas." He said he would present the Education Department budget plan to the Legislative Council the following Tuesday.

Dr. Warren Hill presented Arch Ford with a plaque containing a resolution of praise adopted the past month by the executive committee of the national Education Commission. Ford was a charter member of the executive committee, and the resolution praised him for "his leadership in education, which has extended beyond the geographic boundaries of the state of Arkansas." Copies of the resolution were also given to Clinton and the Arkansas legislature. Several department employees and former employees participated in a "toast and roast" session in Ford's honor as well.[437]

Former governor and U.S. senator Dale Bumpers sent a telegram to Arch Ford on November 28, 1978, sending regrets that he could not attend the Christmas dinner. In it, he said, "How do you roast a man whose life has been dedicated to making life better and more pleasant for everyone?...I would be willing to roast his critics but he has none."[438]

Ford received many letters of congratulations upon his retirement, but the following comment was particularly interesting. Ed Speaker of Conway, an old friend of Arch Ford, wrote the following in a December 2, 1978, letter: "I think one of the greatest things that you have done over the period of years of our friendship is that you have always remained the same Arch Ford."[439]

In a 1977 interview, Ford said this about his years at the Department of Education: "I don't really know how I've survived all these years. I didn't come here with any intention of staying, really. I've thoroughly enjoyed it. I love my job; I love education. I would rather be head of this department than be governor."[440]

Earl Willis, the consultant Arch Ford had hired to help schools

during desegregation fourteen years earlier, was chosen as interim director. Willis had been associate director for finance in the department for the previous seven years before he was named to temporarily replace Ford. Thirty people had applied for Ford's job.[441]

Arch and Ruby Ford at their home on Horseshoe Mountain in 1970. *Photo courtesy of Joe T. Ford*

Farm and Family

Arch and his wife, Ruby, had a 123-acre farm on Horseshoe Mountain, west of Greenbrier. In 1966, they built a ranch-style house there. Horseshoe Mountain was where Ruby had been raised, and many family members lived around them. They had thirteen head of cattle and a dog named Missy. He was a deacon and taught Sunday school at Bethlehem Baptist Church. She started the vacation Bible school program there.

Ruby Ford was known for her cooking, especially her chicken and dressing and hot rolls. Charlotte Roberts, her cousin, said, "Whenever there was a death...she was right there with the chicken and dressing in her big oval roasting pan." Ruby's sister, Jimmie Lee Gean, concurred, "She was a great cook. That's all they talked about up at that church." She also was ready to throw a shower for anyone at the church who was getting married or having a baby.[442]

Charlotte's family often ate Sunday dinner at the Ford house. She recalls that they "always had a good time visiting in the afternoon around the big fireplace in their home if it was cool." She said eating lunch at the Fords' home was one of her kids' biggest joys.[443] Scott Ford, Arch's grandson, remembers the "uproarious laughter as background noise" when he went to his grandparents' home. At the dinner table, they talked about politics and people.[444]

Property Tax Relief and Rollback Amendment

In 1980, Arch Ford served as the chairman of the Faulkner County petition drive campaign to get the Property Tax Relief and Rollback Amendment (proposed Amendment 59) put on the ballot. The amendment would protect property owners by reducing local millage rates to a level that would provide the same amount of tax revenues the local government had the year before the reassessment.[445] The amendment was approved by voters in November, and it reduced property taxes by providing for adjustment and rollback of millage rates when assessed property values rise by more than 10%.

Health Issues

In late 1981 and early 1982, Arch Ford spent several months in Baptist Medical Center after experiencing hallucinations and suffering some kind of attack, possibly a stroke.[446] Scott Ford later said the attack was the result of too much insulin and that Arch was in a diabetic coma for a while.[447] Ford remained healthy for a while after that but eventually had to go live at Johnson's Meadowlake Nursing Home in Conway. He passed away there on June 5, 1987.

The *Arkansas Gazette* writer who reported Ford's death began the article with this: "His low-key approach, general avoidance of political controversy, ability to get along with legislators and local school officials as well as with governors made him one of the most durable state executive officials in modern times."[448]

His administrative assistant, Dorothy Gillam, said he would be remembered as a "compassionate, caring person, a strong advocate for education and a man who loved his family above everything."[449]

Jim Wooten, who served on the board of the Arkansas Council on Economic Education and was a longtime friend of Ford, said, "Arch Ford is one of the most compassionate individuals I have ever encountered. He has a commanding presence but one of compassion for Arkansas and education. He taught me that if it's right, it's right and you stand for it. He is one of the most humble individuals I ever encountered. He was a man of great faith which played a tremendous role in his life and the people he touched."[450]

David Pryor, who by that time was serving in the U.S. Senate, had this to say about the legacy that Arch Ford left in Arkansas: "Arch Ford was my friend and over the years he was the friend of thousands of students and teachers and school administrators—people who may not have known him personally but who benefited from his long years of service and dedication. I don't know anyone who has left a personal stamp on the state as long-lasting as Arch Ford's is on public education. We will all miss his sense of humor and his sensitivity to state history and politics."[451]

Chapter 16: The Legacy Lives On

Arkansas education has long been criticized for being below par when compared to other states. Commissioner Arch Ford's response to the criticism was to have the critics look at how much Arkansas was investing in education despite the low per capita income in the state. Arkansas had one of the lowest per capita incomes in the country, and yet it had made great advances in education since 1948. Arkansas education had come a long way during Ford's time in the Department of Education.

Funding a Quality Education Program

During Arch Ford's tenure, the Department of Education's budget rose from $30.6 million in 1954-55 to $425 million in 1978-79. The amount allocated to education was over half of the entire state budget. The number of school districts in the state decreased to 382 by 1978, and it was anticipated that the Quality Education Act that Arch Ford had crafted would decrease that number even further by the deadline that had been set in 1979. With fewer facilities and better use of resources, the children of Arkansas could receive higher-quality education. The average teachers' salaries were around $14,970 a year by the time Ford retired, and all Arkansas certified teachers had at least a bachelor's degree. Many also had master's degrees, and a few even had doctorates.

Bill Clinton, Mike Huckabee, and those that followed as governor of Arkansas built on the foundation that Ford established. Under Clinton, class sizes were reduced so that teachers could be more effective. Teachers' salaries were raised significantly, and teacher quality was improved through new requirements for teacher training and professional development. The Department of Education expanded to provide curriculum standards and resources for each discipline. Recently, a teacher evaluation system was implemented to encourage teachers to constantly improve what they do in the classroom. The average teacher's salary for Arkansas in 2014 was $48,017. It still has not caught up with the national average, but it is still respectable considering that the 2014 average per capita income for Arkansas was $36,423.[452]

Although the Arkansas Educational Television Network (AETN) was originally designed to provide supplementary instruction to classrooms across the state, it now provides a variety of educational programs for all ages—twenty-four hours a day, seven days a week. In addition, AETN now provides Internet-delivered education to Arkansas teachers as part of the Department of Education's efforts to increase teacher quality and provide training in effective instructional strategies.

Opening Doors to a Better Future

Arch Ford cared very much for the children of Arkansas. He saw education as the door to a better future. He had seen how a bit of education and training helped the young men in the CCC camp go out with confidence to find jobs so they could earn a living and support their families. He believed that a statewide vocational-technical education system could provide the same opportunities to the thousands of young people in Arkansas who did not go to college. By the time he retired, there were twenty-three vocational-technical schools within driving distance of anyone who needed to gain or improve their vocational or technical skills. He also saw the benefits of community colleges and helped establish several of them during his career.

Equal Educational Opportunities

Arch Ford strove to provide equal educational opportunities for all of the children of Arkansas. By leading Arkansas through the desegregation process, he was able to help create unitary school districts throughout the state that could provide equal educational opportunities to all children.

He led the charge to change Arkansas's constitution so that five-year-olds and also adults could receive state-funded educational services. Today, kindergarten is mandatory in the state of Arkansas. The state is now even providing pre-kindergarten services to the more disadvantaged children in the state. Arkansas today has a strong adult education program to assist those who need to complete their high school education or improve their technical skills.

Finally, Ford helped the state assume responsibility for the education of all students who had cognitive or intellectual impairments or were developmentally behind their peers. Today, the Department of Education oversees a massive special education program. Districts provide a variety of services, including resource rooms and self-contained classrooms, and also "inclusion" classes in which special education students are placed into a regular academic classroom with a special education teacher assisting the regular classroom teacher in providing individualized and differentiated instruction. Arch Ford's goal of providing equal educational opportunities to all Arkansas children had expanded to include those with intellectual disabilities and developmental delays.

Economic Education

Arch Ford initially encouraged the establishment of an economic education program in the state as a positive way to combat the spread of communist ideas. He felt that if students understood the basic concepts of a free enterprise market economy, they would better understand the dangers that a communist or socialist economic system posed. The Arkansas Council on Economic Education (now Economics Arkansas) is still providing training to hundreds of classroom teachers so that they can teach concepts of economics to children at all grade levels. It is still important that students understand how the economy works so that they can make better choices for themselves and for their communities. The Arkansas General Assembly recently required all students to have a semester class in economics before graduation. A unit of personal finance must also be taught so that these students can make better choices about their financial resources and careers.

The educational system of Arkansas made great advances during the tenure of Commissioner Arch Ford. He took an underfunded, inadequate system and developed it into a system that could provide quality education to all the children and adults in the state of Arkansas. At the end of his tenure, he left a strong foundation that has allowed Arkansas to continue to make gains and be a leader in developing quality educational programs.

Notes

1 National Education Association, www.nea.org (accessed March 20, 2016).

2 John L. Ward, "Arch W. Ford: A Quiet Survivor of the Political Maelstrom," *Log Cabin Democrat*, January 10, 1979.

3 Loyd D. Ryan, "School Consolidation: A Giant Step for Learning," *Log Cabin Democrat Weekender*, March 9, 1979.

4 Fay Williams, "Introducing Archie Ford, State Commissioner of Education," *Arkansas Democrat Sunday Magazine*, July 19, 1953.

5 Ward, "Arch W. Ford: A Quiet Survivor."

6 Arch E. Pearson, "Memories of the Wooster Community," *Faulkner Facts and Fiddlings* 6 (1964): 86.

7 Kathy Trower, "Road Trips: Wooster Is an Integral Part of Faulkner County, Arkansas," *Arkansas Democrat-Gazette River Valley and Ozark Edition*, July 18, 1999, 6R.

8 Pearson, "The Wooster Community," 85.

9 Fay Williams, "Archie Ford, State Commissioner of Education," in *Arkansans of the Year, 1951–54* (Little Rock: C. C. Allard and Associates, 1954), 80.

10 "It's the Durable Arch Ford and His Door Is Always Open," *Nashville News*, April 12, 1977.

11 Ibid.

12 *ASTC Bulletin* 1922–25.

13 *ASTC Scroll* 1925.

14 Williams, "Introducing Archie Ford," 80.

15 Ibid.

16 Ibid., 81

17 Ibid.

18 *ASTC Scroll* 1928.

19 Williams, "State Commissioner of Education," 81

20 Ibid., 83

21 Ibid.

22 "Excellent Appointment," *Arkansas Democrat* editorial, January 17, 1953.

23 Kay Marmon Danielson, *Jacksonville, Arkansas* (Mount Pleasant, SC: Arcadia Publishing, 2000).

24 Old State House Museum Associates, "Exhibit: The Civilian Conservation Corps in Arkansas," *Faulkner Facts and Fiddlings* (1995): 41.

25 Joseph M. Speakman, "Into the Woods: The First Year of Civilian Conservation Corps," *Prologue* 38, no. 3 (Fall 2006).

26 Howard W. Oxley, "Education in Civilian Conservation Corps Camps," http://catalog. hathitrust.org/Record/003240357 (accessed March 13, 2016).

27 Sandra Taylor Smith, "The Civilian Conservation Corps in Arkansas 1933–1942," Arkansas Historic Preservation Program.

28 Williams, "State Commissioner of Education."

29 "It's the Durable Arch Ford."

30 Ibid.

31 Ibid.

32 Arch Ford, "Leaders in Education," *Education Newsmagazine* (February 1967).

33 "Ford Slated to Be New School Head," *Arkansas Democrat*, January 5, 1953.

34 Ibid.

35 "Career Man Directing Education Department," *Arkansas Democrat*, January 9, 1955.

36 Bill Harwood, "Arch Ford," in *School Days: Contemporary Views on Arkansas Education* (Little Rock: Winthrop Rockefeller Foundation, 1978), 90.

37 "A Survivor in the Spoils Jungle: Veteran Educator Enjoys Relaxing Around Home," *Arkansas Gazette*, January 10, 1979.

38 "Arch Ford's Recipe," *Arkansas Democrat*, October 3, 1977.

39 Ibid.

40 Van A. Tyson, "Education Leader Is Veteran on Job: Ford Has Headed His Department for 21 Years," *Arkansas Democrat*, August 12, 1974.

41 "Arch Ford's Recipe."

42 "Ford Slated to Be New School Head."

43 "Run of the News: A School Man for the Top Education Job," *Arkansas Democrat*, January 7, 1953.

44 "Excellent Appointment," *Arkansas Democrat*, January 7, 1953.

45 Williams, "Introducing Archie Ford."

46 Williams, "State Commissioner of Education."

47 Ibid.

48 Ibid.

49 Williams, "Introducing Archie Ford."

50 "Education Department Goes on TV," *Arkansas Gazette*, November 29, 1959.

51 "Department of Education Publishes Newsmagazine," *Arkansas Democrat*, March 7, 1963.

52 "Countermove to Save Ford's Job Fails; Faubus Voices Sympathy," *Arkansas Gazette*, December 9, 1960.

53 "'Oust Ford' Plan Wins ALC Okay," *Arkansas Gazette*, December 8, 1960.

54 "Countermove to Save Ford's Job Fails."

55 "Jones Denies Role in Vote Against Ford," *Arkansas Gazette*, December 11, 1960.

56 "Board, Faubus Oppose Move to Oust Ford," *Arkansas Gazette*, December 13, 1960.

57 "Van Dalsem and the Education Proviso," *Arkansas Gazette*, December 18, 1960.

58 "Committee Removes Bar to Arch Ford's Education Position," *Arkansas Gazette*, February 7, 1961.

59 "Van Dalsem Off on a Trip, Ford Pulls Comeback," *Arkansas Gazette*, February 12, 1961.

60 Roy Reed, "House Rejects Ford Pay Raise: Van Dalsem Persists, Wins His Vendetta," *Arkansas Gazette*, March 7, 1961.

61 "A Survivor in the Spoils Jungle."

62 "Honorary Doctorate for Two," *Baptist Magazine*, May 1, 1962.

63 "Ford Asked to Explain Inaction," *Arkansas Democrat*, November 22, 1953.

64 "Career Man Directing Education Department."

65 "Education Department to Expand: Addition of Five Supervisors Would Raise Federal Aid," *Arkansas Democrat*, January 5, 1959.

66 "State Board Revises Setup in Education," *Arkansas Gazette*, August 29, 1966.

67 "Reorganization Reverses 97 Years of Traditions," *Arkansas Gazette*, February 7, 1971.

68 Ibid.

69 "Education Department to Complete Its Move," *Arkansas Democrat*, August 29, 1969.

70 "State Complex to Honor Ford," *Arkansas Gazette*, May 20, 1969.

71 "Education Department Considered Too Small to Help 385 Districts," *Arkansas Gazette*, July 3, 1976.

72 "Former Education Department Director, Mr. Ford, Dies at 81," *Log Cabin Democrat*, June 5, 1987.

73 Ibid.

74 "Freedoms Foundation Will Honor A.W. Ford for Work in Education," *Arkansas Gazette*, May 1, 1964.

75 "Leaders in Education: A.W. Ford," *Education* 83 (May 1963): 570.

76 "Arkansas Creed," *Education Newsmagazine* (October 1972).

77 "It's the Durable Arch Ford."

78 Dorothy Gillam interview by Gabe Gentry for Economics Arkansas, April 2015.

79 "50 Years on Job, Education Agency Aide Praised as Gem," *Arkansas Democrat-Gazette*, June 28, 2015.

80 Dorothy Gillam interview by Gabe Gentry.

81 Calvin R. Ledbetter, "The Fight For School Consolidation in Arkansas, 1946–1948," *Arkansas Historical Quarterly* 65 (Spring 2006): 4.

82 Ibid., 5.

83 Ibid., 7.

84 Ibid., 9.

85 Ibid., 12.

86 "Ford Announces that He'll Retire As Education Director," *Log Cabin Democrat*, September 8, 1978.

87 "A Survivor in the Spoils Jungle."

88 "Ford Sees Finances as Top Problem," *Arkansas Democrat*, June 6, 1954.

89 "Ford Says Plan for Equalization Excels Cherry's," *Arkansas Gazette*, March 6, 1955.

90 "GACE Session Maps Strategy for School Aid," *Arkansas Gazette*, December 1, 1956.

91 "Faubus Sees School Chaos if Tax Killed," *Arkansas Gazette*, May 9, 1957.

92 "State May Get Federal Funds for Education," *Arkansas Gazette*, September 9, 1958.

93 "Vast Improvement in Schools Coming Soon, Ford Says," *Arkansas Gazette*, August 22, 1965.

94 Ibid.

95 "Arkansas Taking a Positive View on Education," *Arkansas Gazette*, January 30, 1966.

96 "State Relieved of Pressure," *Arkansas Gazette*, March 22, 1973.

97 "Ford Says Schools Can't Look for Help from Legislature," *Arkansas Gazette*, February 4, 1976.

98 Ibid.

99 Ibid.

100 "Pay Raise for Educators in State Averages $987," *Arkansas Gazette*, February 12, 1976.

101 "School Bill Goes to Pryor," *Arkansas Gazette*, March 2, 1977.

102 "Educators Back School Report," *Arkansas Gazette*, August 25, 1978.

103 Jim Wooten interview with Gabe Gentry for Economics Arkansas, April 2015

104 Bobbie Forster, "Amazing Progress in Education in Decade Cited by Commissioner," *Arkansas Democrat*, March 24, 1959.

105 "Appropriations for School Funds Passed by Senate," *Arkansas Gazette*, November 19, 1977.

106 "State 5th in Proportionate Support of Schools," *Arkansas Gazette*, June 5, 1960.

107 "4.4% of Teachers Lack Degrees, State Survey Shows," *Arkansas Gazette*, October 18, 1966.

108 Roy Bosson, "Tightening of Teacher Rules Hinted: Survey Shows 650 Still Lack 2 Years' College Training," *Arkansas Democrat*, August 6, 1953.

109 Matilda Tuohey, "Ax Swings High and Low in Education Department," *Arkansas Gazette*, June 14, 1955.

110 "Faubus Calls GACE to Its Second Job; Improve Teaching," *Arkansas Gazette*, May 10, 1957.

111 Bobbie Forster, "Amazing Progress of Education."

112 Ernest Valachovic, "State Educators Seek to Improve Teachers' Caliber," *Arkansas Gazette*, April 14, 1959.

113 "Teachers in Arkansas Schools Are Acquiring More Education," *Arkansas Gazette*, December 11, 1960.

114 A. W. Ford, "Arkansas Education Proud of 'Recognition,'" *Arkansas Democrat*, January 27, 1963.

115 "State Board Moves to Raise Standards in Teacher Hiring," *Arkansas Gazette*, June 10, 1963.

116 "State Board Approves 60-Hour Plan for School Administrators," *Arkansas Gazette*, September 9, 1963.

117 "4.4% of Teachers Lack Degrees."

118 "Arkansas Totals Teachers' Degrees," *Commercial Appeal*, July 12, 1967.

119 "Most Teachers Have a Degree," *Arkansas Gazette*, March 10, 1970.

120 "Standards Revised for Certification of State Teachers," *Arkansas Gazette*, March 10, 1970.

121 "Ruling Means that Teachers Get an Extra $600,000," *Arkansas Gazette*, August 5, 1953.

122 Bobbie Forster, "Amazing Progress of Education."

123 "Ford Spurns Raise Unless Teachers Also Get More," *Arkansas Gazette*, March 8, 1955.

124 "Pay Raise for Educators Averages $987," *Arkansas Gazette*, February 12, 1976.

125 "School Bill Goes to Pryor," *Arkansas Gazette*, March 2, 1977.

126 Ward, "Arch W. Ford: A Quiet Survivor."

127 Arch Ford, "More School Consolidation," *Arkansas Democrat*, June 25, 1953.

128 "Reorganization Plan Stirs Fuss in GACE: Ford Leads Opposition to Plan of Penalties for Balky Districts," *Arkansas Gazette*, June 21, 1956.

129 "School Unit Study in Every County Okayed by Senate," *Arkansas Gazette*, February 14, 1963.

130 "School Trends Noted by Ford," *Commercial Appeal*, April 4, 1963.

131 "Closing of State's 'Weak' Schools Suggested by Ford," *Arkansas Gazette*, March 10, 1964.

132 "Consolidation Defeated by a Big Margin," *Arkansas Gazette*, November 9, 1966.

133 "School Quality Bill Introduced," *Arkansas Gazette*, January 14, 1969.

134 "Quality Education Act, With Jones' Change Passed 26-1 in Senate," *Arkansas Gazette*, March 2, 1969.

135 "Survivor in the Spoils Jungle."

136 "All Schools Able to Run for 9 Months," *Arkansas Gazette*, March 23, 1958.

137 "Divided Term Schools Draw 500 Students," *Arkansas Gazette*, May 31, 1961.

138 "Education Council Set Up in Arkansas: Group Will Deal With Secondary Level Problems," Associated Press, December 15, 1957, in Arch Ford Collection, University of Arkansas Libraries Special Collections.

139 "Educators to Study Curricula Revisions: Agriculture, Home Economics to Be De-Emphasized," *Commercial Appeal*, January 4, 1958.

140 "Crash Program on Science Vetoed by Ford," *Arkansas Gazette*, January 28, 1958.

141 "Arkansas Takes New Interest in Curriculum: Educators Report Parents Are Concerned with Johnny's Subjects," *Commercial Appeal*, March 1, 1958.

142 "Ford Praises Legislative Acts on Education," *Arkansas Gazette*, March 19, 1963.

143 "Panel Approves Goals Statement for Education," *Arkansas Gazette*, November 10, 1977.

144 "Education Board Adopts Standards for Three Grades," *Arkansas Gazette*, March 14, 1978.

145 "Panel Approves Goals Statement for Education."

146 "Education Board Adopts Standards for Three Grades."

147 "Future of Education Great, Dr. Ford Says," *Daily Banner-News*, January 8, 1975.

148 "Arch Ford's Recipe."

149 Ibid.

150 "Future of Education Great, Dr. Ford Says."

151 "Guidelines on Discipline to Be Sought, Ford Says," *Arkansas Gazette*, January 17, 1975.

152 Ernest Dumas, "Discipline Panel Circulating Rules to Use as a Model," *Arkansas Gazette*, March 18, 1976.

153 "Inequities in Education Up for Study: Survey to Cover Equalization and Segregation Issues," *Arkansas Democrat*, December 14, 1953.

154 "State Committed to Desegregation, Ford Declares," *Arkansas Gazette*, April 2, 1968.

155 Ibid.

156 Ibid.

157 "Separate But Equal Policy Set for Schools," *Arkansas Democrat*, June 14, 1954.

158 Ibid.

159 Ibid.

160 Ken Kaufman, "Arkansas Integration Must Wait, Ford Says," *Arkansas Democrat*, July 1, 1954.

161 Ibid.

162 Ibid.

163 Sam Harris, "State's Pattern to be Set by District Tribunals; Decision Lauded by Most," *Arkansas Gazette*, June 1, 1955.

164 Ibid.

165 "State Committed to Desegregation, Ford Declares," *Arkansas Gazette*, April 2, 1968.

166 "Education Board Considering Plan of Study to Avert 'Little Rocks,'" *Arkansas Gazette*, December 10, 1957.

167 Ibid.

168 "269 Negroes in Integrated Schools," *Arkansas Gazette*, September 30, 1962.

169 "Ford Opposes Racial Rider on School Bill: Tells House Group Whites Also Denied Equal Opportunities," *Arkansas Gazette*, June 19, 1963.

170 Ibid.

171 Ibid.

172 "Seven Times More Negroes Attend Integrated Schools," *Arkansas Gazette*, January 1, 1966.

173 "Education Department Integrated," *Arkansas Gazette*, June 3, 1965.

174 Dorothy Gillam interview by Scott Lunsford for the Pryor Center, August 3, 2011.

175 Dorothy Gillam interview by Gabe Gentry for Economics Arkansas, April 2015.

176 "50 Years on Job, Education Agency Aide Praised as Gem."

177 "Arkansas Swaps Integration Record," *Commercial Appeal*, December 31, 1965.

178 Ibid.

179 "Seven Times More Negroes Attend Integrated Schools."

180 Ibid.

181 "Choice Plans for Schools Under Review," *Arkansas Gazette*, January 11, 1966.

182 "Negro Leader Disputes Ford on Integration," *Arkansas Gazette*, January 29, 1966.

183 Ibid.

184 "U.S. Tells South It Must Speed Up School Integration," *Arkansas Gazette*, March 8, 1966.

185 Ibid.

186 Ibid.

187 Ibid.

188 "Avoiding Political Talk, Ford Says State to Go Forward with Education," *Arkansas Gazette*, September 8, 1966.

189 "Ford Declines Bid to Discuss New Bias Rules," *Arkansas Gazette*, April 12, 1966.

190 "Enforcement Not State Job, Ford Tells Howe," *Arkansas Gazette*, July 6, 1966.

191 "HEW Tells South 1969 Is Deadline for Desegregation," *Arkansas Gazette*, November 9, 1967.

192 "Ford Views School Integration Order," *Arkansas Democrat*, November 9, 1967.

193 "New Desegregation Directive May Affect About a Fourth of State Schools, Ford Says," *Arkansas Gazette*, November 9, 1967.

194 "Ford Names 1ˢᵗ Consultant on School Desegregation; He's a Veteran Educator," *Arkansas Gazette*, April 16, 1968.

195 "53,000 Arkansas Negroes Now are Attending School in Desegregated Districts," *Arkansas Gazette*, September 17, 1969.

196 "Letting Governor Take Over School Unwise, Ford Says," *Arkansas Gazette*, November 1, 1969.

197 "6 Districts in State Refusing to Comply, Ford Informs U.S.," *Arkansas Gazette*, May 9, 1970.

198 Jerol Garrison, "Cooperation Is Ordered in Planning," *Arkansas Gazette*, July 10, 1970.

199 Jerol Garrison, "16 Years after Ruling, Integration Nears Completion in State Schools," *Arkansas Gazette*, August 30, 1970.

200 "Ford Pledges Help with Adjustment to Desegregation," *Arkansas Gazette*, May 2, 1972.

201 "State Board of Education Approves Plan to Improve Job Opportunities for Blacks, Women," *Arkansas Gazette*, March 3, 1974.

202 Harwood, "Arch Ford," in *School Days: Contemporary Views on Arkansas Education*, 90.

203 "Council Orders Trade School at Little Rock," *Arkansas Gazette*, August 17, 1957.

204 "A. W. Ford Plugs Area Training," *Arkansas Union Farmer* (January 1957).

205 "Cloud-Soaring Vocational Plan," *Arkansas Democrat*, January 30, 1957.

206 "Board Seeking Cities' Applications for Vocational-Technical Teen Schools," *Arkansas Gazette*, July 10, 1957.

207 "School Seekers Heard," *Arkansas Gazette*, August 2, 1957.

208 "Council Orders Trade School at Little Rock."

209 Ibid.

210 Ibid.

211 Ibid.

212 "Won't Interfere in Picking School Site, Faubus Says," *Arkansas Gazette*, August 22, 1957.

213 "Benefits Told of Little Rock School Site," *Arkansas Gazette*, August 22, 1957.

214 "Won't Interfere in Picking School Site, Faubus Says."

215 Leroy Donald, "Trade Schools May Become Third System," *Arkansas Gazette*, October 4, 1961.

216 "Technical School Has 224 Enrollees," *Arkansas Gazette*, October 14, 1959.

217 "Pine Bluff School Draws 509 Students," *Commercial Appeal*, February 28, 1960.

218 Donald, "Trade Schools May Become Third System."

219 "State Vocational Training Increase Needed, Funds Lacking, Ford Says," *Arkansas Gazette*, September 12, 1961.

220 Donald, "Trade Schools May Become Third System."

221 "Morrilton Plugs Itself as Site for Tech School," *Arkansas Gazette*, February 9, 1962.

222 "Faubus Praises Morrilton as Site of Vocational School," *Arkansas Gazette*, February 20, 1962.

223 Ernest Valachovic, "Fuss Continues on Site Choice for New School," *Arkansas Gazette*, February 25, 1962.

224 "Pine Bluff Man to Head School at Morrilton," *Arkansas Gazette*, March 13, 1962.

225 "Cooling Units Set for School at Petit Jean," *Arkansas Gazette*, March 11, 1963.

226 "Trade School at Morrilton Dedicated," *Arkansas Gazette*, August 26, 1963.

227 "Training School to Be Available for All in State," *Arkansas Gazette*, July 7, 1963.

228 "Trade Schools Announced for Eight Areas," *Arkansas Gazette*, June 15, 1965.

229 "Trade School Committee to be Named," *Arkansas Gazette*, September 11, 1963.

230 Ibid.

231 "New State Vocational School Is Sought by Several Cities," *Arkansas Gazette*, November 9, 1963.

232 "Trade Schools Announced for Eight Areas," *Arkansas Gazette*, June 15, 1965.

233 "8 Tech Schools Named; 4 Get List of Courses," *Arkansas Gazette*, July 21, 1965.

234 "Trade School Bid Openings Set for May 17," *Arkansas Gazette*, March 15, 1966.

235 "Vo-Tech Here Gets New Name," *Pine Bluff Commercial*, March 18, 1966.

236 "Course at 6 Trade Schools Ready for Board's Approval," *Arkansas Gazette*, May 18, 1966.

237 "Tech School a Big Help, Pryor Says," *Arkansas Gazette*, July 6, 1966.

238 "Education Board Decides to Reject Vo-tech Changes," *Arkansas Gazette*, June 8, 1970.

239 "Average Pay Raise of $423 Budgeted for State Teachers," *Arkansas Gazette*, June 14, 1971.

240 "5,300 People Attend Dedication Ceremonies," *Log Cabin Democrat*, December 3, 1973.

241 "Mobile Machine Shop Training Unit," *Education Newsmagazine* (October 1970).

242 "Mobile Education," *Arkansas Gazette*, January 7, 1973.

243 "State Prisons Get $200,000 for Education," *Arkansas Gazette*, March 24, 1970.

244 "Ford Supports Move to Form Two Year Colleges," *Arkansas Gazette*, March 19, 1964.

245 "Education Board, Staff Will Fight Junior College Plan," *Arkansas Gazette*, September 12, 1972.

246 "Kindergarten Program Backed by Commissioner," *Log Cabin Democrat*, November 15, 1967.

247 "Pulaski Vocational Technical School to Open at Its New Location January 19," *Arkansas Gazette*, January 11, 1976

248 "A Survivor in the Spoils Jungle."

249 "Arkansas on Alert against 'Red' Material in Public School Books," Arkansas Democrat, September 27, 1953.

250 "'Left Wing' Textbook Probe Set," Arkansas Democrat, November 22, 1953.

251 Roy Reed, Faubus: The Life and Times of an American Prodigal (Fayetteville: University of Arkansas Press, 1997), 261.

252 Ibid., 274

253 Ibid.

254 Joe Ford interview by Gabe Gentry for Economics Arkansas, April 2015

255 George and Mildred Fersh, Bessie Moore: A Biography (Little Rock: August House, 1986), 84.

256 Ibid., 83

257 Ibid., 85–86.

258 "Tuesday Meeting Will Form Economic Education Council," Arkansas Gazette, February 25, 1962.

259 George and Mildred Fersh, Bessie Moore: A Biography.

260 Ibid., 87.

261 Ibid., 92.

262 Ibid., 92–93.

263 "Economic Council Sponsors Three Sessions for Teachers," Arkansas Gazette, March 14, 1963.

264 "Who's Who in U.S. Business to Conduct State Seminar," Arkansas Gazette, June 9, 1963.

265 "100 Educators Registered as Economics Courses Begin," Arkansas Gazette, June 24, 1963.

266 "Economic Council Sponsors Three Sessions for Teachers."

267 "State's Economic Education Promoted by Sears, Roebuck," Arkansas Gazette, June 19, 1963.

268 George and Mildred Fersh, Bessie Moore: A Biography, 101.

269 "Ford Emphasizes Role of Economics in State Schools," Arkansas Gazette, July 13, 1963.

270 George and Mildred Fersh, Bessie Moore: A Biography, 87.

271 Ibid., 103.

272 Ibid., 104.

273 "ASTC Gets $8,000 Grant to Hold Economics Course," Arkansas Gazette, March 24, 1965.

274 George and Mildred Fersh, Bessie Moore: A Biography, 137–38.

275 Ibid., 86.

276 "LR District May Get Experimental Program in Economic Education," *Arkansas Gazette*, January 5, 1966.

277 "State a Leader in Teaching of Economics," *Arkansas Gazette*, January 19, 1966.

278 "Arkansas No. 1 in Economic Education," *Arkansas Gazette*, August 5, 1966.

279 "State Teachers Win Awards in Economics," *Arkansas Gazette*, October 26, 1967.

280 "Ford Again Elected to Economic Group," *Arkansas Gazette*, November 13, 1968.

281 George and Mildred Fersh, *Bessie Moore: A Biography*, 110.

282 Ibid., 110.

283 Ibid., 111.

284 10th Anniversary of Arkansas Council on Economic Education program at Economics Arkansas.

285 "Economics Education Center Named for HSC President," *Arkansas Gazette*, August 15, 1969.

286 Arkansas Educational Television Network, www.aetn.org/history (accessed March 20, 2016).

287 "Educational TV Group to Meet," *Arkansas Democrat*, July 8, 1958.

288 Arkansas Educational Television Network, www.aetn.org/history (accessed March 20, 2016).

289 Ibid.

290 Ibid.

291 "Tyler to Head TV Commission" *Arkansas Gazette*, March 2, 1962.

292 "KATV's Offer Accepted; State Reveals Program for Education Network," *Arkansas Gazette*, March 23, 1962.

293 "AETN—'Zoom!' to 'I, Claudius': State Blanketed with Programs," *Arkansas Gazette*, March 9, 1978.

294 "House Okays Bills on Educational TV," *Arkansas Gazette*, March 8, 1963.

295 "Education TV May Start Early," *Arkansas Gazette*, April 5, 1963.

296 "Dean of A&M Picked to Direct Educational TV," *Arkansas Gazette*, April 21, 1963.

297 "Educational TV Target Date Set as July, 1964," *Arkansas Gazette*, March 20, 1963.

298 "Ford Defends Separate Board for School TV," *Arkansas Gazette*, June 25, 1963.

299 Ibid.

300 "Plans for $750,000 Educational TV Network Are Unveiled," *Commercial Appeal*, July 6, 1964.

301 Arkansas TV Pacts Ok'd After Conway Provides Push," *Commercial Appeal*, February 24, 1966.

302 "Director Sees ETV on Air by October 1," *Arkansas Gazette*, March 2, 1966.

303 Arkansas Educational Television Network, www.aetn.org/history (accessed March 20, 2016).

304 Cecil McDermott letter, November 5, 1974, in Arch Ford Collection, scrapbook 50, University of Arkansas Libraries Special Collections.

305 Sid McMath letter, March 6, 1975, in Arch Ford Collection, scrapbook 51, University of Arkansas Libraries Special Collections.

306 "Color ETV Programs to Be Closer After Antenna Is Installed Today," *Arkansas Gazette*, February 23, 1972.

307 Ibid.

308 Ibid.

309 "Reorganization Reverses 97 Years of Traditions," *Arkansas Gazette*, February 7, 1971.

310 "Aid to Education Leads List," *Arkansas Gazette*, April 8, 1973.

311 Arkansas Educational Television Network, www.aetn.org/history (accessed March 20, 2016).

312 "AETN—'Zoom!' to 'I, Claudius': State Blanketed With Programs."

313 Ibid.

314 Ibid.

315 Arkansas Educational Television Network, www.aetn.org/history (accessed March 20, 2016).

316 Ibid.

317 Elizabeth Shores, "The Arkansas Children's Colony at Conway: A Springboard for Federal Policy on Special Education," *Arkansas Historical Quarterly* 57, no. 4 (1998): 408.

318 Reed, *Faubus: The Life and Times of An American Prodigal*.

319 Shores, "The Arkansas Children's Colony at Conway.

320 Ibid.

321 Ibid., 414.

322 Sandi Bramlett, "Human Development Center," in *Faulkner County: Its Land and People*, (Conway, AR: River Road Press, 1986), 271.

323 Ibid., 415.

324 Ibid., 417.

325 "Training Teachers for the Retarded," *Arkansas Democrat*, August 3, 1955.

326 Ibid., 410–11.

327 Ibid., 418–19.

328 Ibid., 420.

329 Ibid., 424.

330 Ibid., 426.

331 Ibid., 427.

332 John L.Ward,"Special Education Needs Charting of New Course," *Arkansas Democrat*, February 16, 1961.

333 "45,000 Youth Are Listed With Defects, AED Reports," *Arkansas Gazette*, February 2, 1962.

334 "3 Pct. of State's Children Retarded, Report Shows," *Arkansas Gazette*, March 8, 1962.

335 Ibid.

336 A. W. Ford, "Arkansas Education Proud of 'Recognition' in 1962," *Arkansas Democrat*, January 27, 1963.

337 "Plan to Help Handicapped Approved," *Arkansas Gazette*, September 12, 1967.

338 Shores, "The Arkansas Children's Colony at Conway," 431.

339 "Special Education Needed for Many Children," *Arkansas Democrat*, November 3, 1969.

340 Ibid.

341 "Ford to Urge Public School for Retarded," *Arkansas Gazette*, July 15, 1972.

342 Ibid.

343 "Aid to Education Leads List," *Arkansas Gazette*, April 8, 1973.

344 "Big School Districts Urged to Establish Handicapped Plans," *Arkansas Gazette*, January 7, 1975.

345 Ibid.

346 Ibid.

347 Ibid.

348 Ibid.

349 Ibid.

350 "Schools Face Financial Bind in Classes for Handicapped," *Arkansas Gazette*, March 7, 1976.

351 "Special Education and How it Works," *Arkansas Gazette*, January 2, 1977.

352 "Board Adopts Plan for Education of Handicapped," *Arkansas Gazette*, September 13, 1977.

353 "State Losing Funds," *Arkansas Gazette*, December 13, 1977.

354 Ernest Valachovic, "Educators Study State Operation of Kindergartens," *Arkansas Gazette*, June 18, 1961.

355 "Ford Says State Must Plan for Kindergarten Program," *Arkansas Gazette*, December 5, 1962.

356 "Governor Says He Favors Kindergarten for Public," *Arkansas Gazette*, December 30, 1964.

357 "Ford Says Ratings Misleading Public on School Quality," *Arkansas Gazette*, December 21, 1966.

358 "Kindergartens Run by Aid Are Approved," *Arkansas Gazette*, October 23, 1965.

359 "Ford Says Ratings Misleading Public on School Quality."

360 "State Schedules Adult Schooling Trial Program," *Arkansas Gazette*, July 14, 1961.

361 Arch Ford, "Kindergarten Amendment," *Education Newsmagazine* (October 1968).

362 "Kindergarten Program Backed by Commissioner," *Log Cabin Democrat*, November 15, 1967.

363 "$4 Million Sought for Kindergartens in New Biennium," *Arkansas Democrat*, October 9, 1970.

364 "Kindergarten Bill Stirs Disorder," *Arkansas Gazette*, April 2, 1971.

365 "The Demise of the Kindergarten and Bail-Reform Bills," *Arkansas Democrat*, April 7, 1971.

366 "Bumpers' Request for Kindergarten Turned Down," *Arkansas Gazette*, January 4, 1973.

367 "Legislative Battle on Kindergarten Set Next Week," *Arkansas Democrat*, January 4, 1973.

368 Ibid.

369 "Legislators Balk at Idea of Public Kindergarten," *Arkansas Democrat*, January 7, 1973.

370 "Kindergarten Bill Favored after Senators Change Vote," *Arkansas Gazette*, January 20, 1973.

371 "Legislators Balk at Idea of Public Kindergarten."

372 Ibid.

373 Ibid.

374 "Kindergarten Bill Signed by Bumpers," *Arkansas Gazette*, February 9, 1973.

375 "Funding Is Voted for Kindergartens, Junior Colleges," *Arkansas Gazette*, April 4, 1973.

376 "Substantial Gains in Arkansas Education," *Arkansas Gazette*, September 23, 1973.

377 "Building Lag Slows Kindergarten Requests," *Arkansas Gazette*, August 13, 1974.

378 Ibid.

379 "School Bill Goes to Pryor," *Arkansas Gazette*, March 2, 1977.

380 "Pryor Got Most Items He Wanted," *Jonesboro Sun*, August 7, 1977.

381 "Table 5.3 Types of state and district requirements for kindergarten entrance and attendance, by state, 2014," https://nces.ed.gov/programs/statereform/tab5_3.asp (accessed March 14, 2016).

382 "Free Textbooks in High School Are Proposed," *Arkansas Gazette*, October 14, 1965.

383 "Free High School Textbooks Come into Limelight Again," *Arkansas Gazette*, March 11, 1962.

384 Ibid.

385 "Free Textbooks in High School Are Proposed."

386 Ibid.

387 "Ford Says State Can Afford Free Textbooks as Well as Raise for Teachers," *Arkansas Gazette*, October 11, 1966.

388 Ibid.

389 "Free Textbooks Recommended if Funds Found," *Arkansas Gazette*, October 12, 1966.

390 "Governor Signs Textbook Bill," *Arkansas Gazette*, March 16, 1967.

391 "Free Textbooks Major Priority, Governor Declares," *Arkansas Gazette*, September 2, 1972.

392 "JBC Approves Appropriation for Textbooks," *Arkansas Gazette*, March 13, 1973.

393 "Committee on Textbooks Approved," *Arkansas Gazette*, March 13, 1973.

394 "Bill Is Planned to Require Fire Marshal Program," *Arkansas Gazette*, December 14, 1958.

395 "Education Act Improves State Department Staff," *Arkansas Gazette*, January 29, 1961.

396 Williams, "Introducing Archie Ford."

397 Ibid., 98.

398 Joe Ford interview by Gabe Gentry for Economics Arkansas, April 2015.

399 Ibid., 184.

400 Ibid., 183.

401 Ibid.

402 Ibid.

403 Joe Ford interview by Gabe Gentry for Economics Arkansas, April 2015.

404 Ibid., 48–49.

405 "Ford Seeks Re-election," *Arkansas Gazette*, March 12, 1972.

406 "Ford Cited as Only State Legislator With 'Perfect' AEA Voting Record," *Arkansas Gazette*, April 22, 1977.

407 David A. Patten and Jeffrey L. Rodengen, *The Legend of Alltel*, (Fort Lauderdale, FL: Write Stuff Syndicate, 2001), 162.

408 Ibid., 163.

409 Ibid., 184–85.

410 Andrew Ross Sorkin and Laura M. Holson, "Verizon Agrees to Buy Alltel for $28.1 Billion," *New York Times*, June 6, 2008.

411 Mark Darrough, "An American Dream for Africa: Scott Ford and the Rwanda Trading Company," June 20, 2011, http://www.sagamoreinstitute.org/library-article/an-american-dream-for-africa-scott-ford-and-the-rwanda-trading-company/ (accessed March 14, 2016).

412 Ibid.

413 Scott Ford interview by Gabe Gentry for Economics Arkansas, April 2015.

414 Joe Ford interview by Gabe Gentry for Economics Arkansas, April 2015

415 Justin Williams Sr., "The Clements of Wooster," *Faulkner Facts and Fiddlings* 21 (1979).

416 Williams, "State Commissioner of Education," 83.

417 Williams, "Introducing Archie Ford."

418 "Centennial: Faulkner County and Conway, 1873–1973," special publication of the *Log Cabin Democrat*, April 21, 1973.

419 "Security Expects to Receive Bids in December," *Log Cabin Democrat*, November 24, 1967.

420 "Security Savings and Loan Financial Statement, June 30, 1968," in Arch Ford Collection scrapbook 24, University of Arkansas Libraries Special Collections.

421 "Security Savings and Loan Names Three Officers," *Log Cabin Democrat*, April 11, 1975.

422 "Johnson to Become President of Security Savings and Loan," *Log Cabin Democrat*, December 13, 1977.

423 "Ford to Run Drive for College's Funds," *Arkansas Gazette*, July 16, 1968.

424 "Church Group Selects Top Arkansas Father," *Stuttgart Daily Leader*, June 18, 1971.

425 "Ford Named 1971 Father by Baptists," *Arkansas Gazette*, June 19, 1971.

426 "Arch W. Ford Honored," *Baptist Trumpet*, August 30, 1978.

427 *The Bulletin*, ASTC alumni newsletter, January 1963, in Arch Ford Collection, University of Arkansas Libraries Special Collections.

428 Joan Shofner, Director of Advancement Research, University of Central Arkansas, email to author, August 28, 2015.

429 "Dr. Ford Stresses Laxing Teacher's Ego," *Newport Independent*, August 30, 1973.

430 Ernest Dumas, "Education Head Will Retire: Ford to Leave Post After 26 Years," *Arkansas Gazette*, September 8, 1978.

431 "Arch Ford Appreciation Day—December 1," *Education Newsmagazine* (November 1978).

432 "Tribute to Dr. A. W. Ford," advertisement for AETN in Arch Ford Collection, scrapbook 73, University of Arkansas Libraries Special Collections.

433 "Joint Resolution 77-76" Joint Interim Committee on Education," in Arch Ford Collection, scrapbook 72, University of Arkansas Libraries Special Collections.

434 Arch Ford Appreciation Day Program document, Arch Ford Collection, scrapbook 73, University of Arkansas Libraries Special Collections.

435 Dorothy Gillam interview by Gabe Gentry for Economics Arkansas, April 2015

436 "Remarks of Bessie B. Moore at Arch Ford Day Program," Arch Ford Collection, scrapbook 73, University of Arkansas Libraries Special Collections.

437 "Ford Subject of Accolades at Yule Dinner," *Arkansas Gazette*, December 11, 1978.

438 Dale Bumpers telegram, November 28, 1978, Arch Ford Collection, scrapbook 73, University of Arkansas Libraries Special Collections.

439 Ed Speaker letter, December 2, 1978, Arch Ford Collection, scrapbook 73, University of Arkansas Libraries Special Collections.

440 "It's the Durable Arch Ford."

441 "Interim Director Is Named for Education Department," *Arkansas Gazette*, December 12, 1978.

442 "Friends, Family Recall Ruby Ford's Good Works," *Log Cabin Democrat*, May 14, 2005.

443 Ibid.

444 Scott Ford interview by Gabe Gentry for Economics Arkansas, April 2015

445 "Yesterdays—25 Years Ago," *Log Cabin Democrat*, May 7, 2005.

446 "Former Education Department Director, Mr. Ford, Dies at 81," *Log Cabin Democrat*, June 5, 1987.

447 Scott Ford interview by Gabe Gentry for Economics Arkansas, April 2015

448 "Former Commissioner of Education Dies at 81," *Arkansas Gazette*, June 6, 1987.

449 Dorothy Gillam interview by Gabe Gentry for Economics Arkansas, April 2015.

450 Jim Wooten interview by Gabe Gentry for Economics Arkansas, April 2015.

451 Ibid.

452 National Education Association, www.nea.org (accessed March 14, 2016).

Bibliography

"3 Pct. of State's Children Retarded, Report Shows." *Arkansas Gazette*, March 8, 1962.

"$4 Million Sought for Kindergartens in New Biennium." *Arkansas Democrat*, October 9, 1970.

"4.4% of Teachers Lack Degrees, State Survey Shows." *Arkansas Gazette*, October 18, 1966.

"6 Districts in State Refusing to Comply, Ford Informs U.S." *Arkansas Gazette*, May 9, 1970.

"8 Tech Schools Named; 4 Get List of Courses." *Arkansas Gazette*, July 21, 1965.

"10th anniversary of the Arkansas Council on Economic Education program at Economics Arkansas."

"50 Years on Job, Education Agency Aide Praised as Gem." *Arkansas Democrat-Gazette*, June 28, 2015.

"100 Educators Registered as Economics Courses Begin." *Arkansas Gazette*, June 24, 1963.

"269 Negroes in Integrated Schools." *Arkansas Gazette*, September 30, 1962.

"5,300 Attend Dedication Ceremonies." *Log Cabin Democrat*, December 3, 1973.

"45,000 Youth Are Listed with Defects." *Arkansas Gazette*, February 2, 1962.

"53,000 Arkansas Negroes Now Are Attending School in Desegregated Districts." *Arkansas Gazette*, September 17, 1969.

"AETN–'Zoom!' to 'I, Claudius': State Blanketed with Programs." *Arkansas Gazette*, March 9, 1978.

"ASTC Gets $8,000 Grant to Hold Economics Courses." *Arkansas Gazette*, March 24, 1965.

"A. W. Ford Plugs Area Training." *Arkansas Union Farmer*, January, 1967.

"Aid to Education Leads List." *Arkansas Gazette*, April 8, 1973.

"All Schools Able to Run for 9 Months." *Arkansas Gazette*, March 23, 1958.

"Appropriations for School Funds Passed By Senate." *Arkansas Gazette*, November 19, 1977.

"Arch Ford's Recipe." *Arkansas Democrat*, October 3, 1977.

"Arkansas Creed." *Education Newsmagazine*, October, 1973.

Arkansas Educational Television Network. www.aetn.org/history (accessed March 20, 2016).

"Arkansas No.1 in Economic Education." *Arkansas Gazette*, August 5, 1966.

"Arkansas on Alert against 'Red' Material in Public School Books." *Arkansas Democrat*, September 27, 1953.

"Arkansas Takes a Positive View on Education." *Arkansas Gazette*, January 30, 1966.

"Arkansas Takes New Interest in Curriculum: Educators Report Parents Are Concerned With Johnny's Subjects." *Commercial Appeal*, March 1, 1958.

Arkansas State Teachers College *Bulletin*, 1922–1925.

Arkansas State Teachers College *Scroll*, 1924, 1925, and 1928.

"Arkansas Totals Teachers' Degrees." *Commercial Appeal*, July 12, 1967.

"Arkansas Swaps Integration Record." *Commercial Appeal*, December 31, 1965.

"Arkansas TV Pacts Ok'd after Conway Provides Push." *Commercial Appeal*, February 24, 1966.

"Average Pay Raise of $423 Budgeted for State Teachers." *Arkansas Gazette*, June 14, 1971.

"Avoiding Political Talk, Ford Says State to Go Forward with Education." *Arkansas Gazette*, September 8, 1966.

"Benefits Told of Little Rock School Site." *Arkansas Gazette*, August 22, 1957.

"Big School Districts Urged to Establish Handicapped Plans." *Arkansas Gazette*, January 2, 1975.

"Bill Is Planned to Require Fire Marshal Program." *Arkansas Gazette*, December 14, 1958.

"Board Adopts Plan for Education of Handicapped." *Arkansas Gazette*, September 13, 1977.

"Board, Faubus Oppose Move to Oust Ford." *Arkansas Gazette*, December 13, 1960.

"Board Seeking Cities' Applications for Vocational-Technical Teen Schools." *Arkansas Gazette*, July 10, 1957.

Bosson, Roy. "Tightening of Teacher Rules Hinted: Survey Shows 650 Still Lack 2 Years' College Training," *Arkansas Democrat*, August 6, 1953.

Bramlett, Sandi. "Human Development Center." *Faulkner County: Its Land and People*. Conway, AR: River Road Press, 1986.

"Building Lag Slows Kindergarten Requests." *Arkansas Gazette*, August 13, 1974.

The Bulletin, ASTC alumni newsletter, January 1963. Arch Ford Collection, University of Arkansas Libraries Special Collections.

"Bumpers' Request for Kindergarten Turned Down." *Arkansas Gazette*, January 4, 1973.

"Career Man Directing Education Department." *Arkansas Democrat*, January 9, 1955.

"Centennial: Faulkner County and Conway, 1873-1973," special publication of *Log Cabin Democrat*, April 21, 1973.

"Choice Plans for Schools Under Review." *Arkansas Gazette*, January 11, 1966.

"Closing of State's 'Weak' Schools Suggested by Ford." *Arkansas Gazette*, March 10, 1964.

"Cloud-Soaring Vocational Plan." *Arkansas Democrat*, January 30, 1957.

"Color ETV Programs to Be Closer after Antenna Is Installed Today." *Arkansas Gazette*, February 23, 1972.

"Committee on Textbooks Approved." *Arkansas Gazette*, March 13, 1973.

"Committee Removes Bar to Arch Ford's Education Position." *Arkansas Gazette*, February 7, 1961.

"Consolidation Defeated by a Big Margin." *Arkansas Gazette*, November 9, 1966.

"Cooling Units Set For School at Petit Jean." *Arkansas Gazette*, March 11, 1963.

"Council Orders Trade School at Little Rock." *Arkansas Gazette*, August 17, 1957.

"Countermove to Save Ford's Job Fails; Faubus Voices Sympathy." *Arkansas Gazette*, December 9, 1960.

"Course at 6 Trade Schools Ready for Board's Approval." *Arkansas Gazette*, May 18, 1966.

"Crash Program on Science Vetoed by Ford." *Arkansas Gazette*, January 28, 1958.

Danielson, Kay Marmon. *Jacksonville, Arkansas*. Mount Pleasant, SC: Arcadia Publishing, 2000.

Darrough, Mark. "An American Dream for Africa: Scott Ford and the Rwanda Trading Company." June 20, 2011, http://www.sagamoreinstitute.org/library-article/an-american-dream-for-africa-scott-ford-and-the-rwanda-trading-company/ (accessed March 14, 2016).

"Dean of A&M Picked to Direct Educational TV." *Arkansas Gazette*, April 21, 1963.

"Department of Education Publishes Newsmagazine." *Arkansas Democrat*, March 7, 1963.

"The Demise of the Kindergarten and Bail-Reform Bills." *Arkansas Democrat*, April 7, 1971.

"Director Sees ETV on Air by October 1." *Arkansas Gazette*, March 2, 1966.

"Divided Term Schools Draw 500 Students." *Arkansas Gazette*, May 31, 1961.

Donald, Leroy. "Trade Schools May Become Third System." *Arkansas Gazette*, October 4, 1961.

"Dr. Ford Stresses Laxing Teacher's Ego." *Newport Independent*, August 30, 1973.

Dumas, Ernest. "Discipline Panel Circulating Rules to Use as Model." *Arkansas Gazette*, March 16, 1976.

"Economic Council Sponsors Three Sessions for Teachers." *Arkansas Gazette*, March 14, 1963.

"Education Act Improves State Department Staff." *Arkansas Gazette*, January 29, 1961.

"Education Board Adopts Standards for Three Grades." *Arkansas Gazette*, March 14, 1978.

"Economic Education Center Named for HSC President." *Arkansas Gazette*, August 15, 1969.

"Education Board Considering Plans of Study to Avert 'Little Rocks.'" *Arkansas Gazette*, December 10, 1957.

"Education Board Decides to Reject Vo-tech Changes." *Arkansas Gazette*, June 8, 1970.

"Education Board, Staff Will Fight Junior College Plan." *Arkansas Gazette*, September 12, 1972.

"Education Council Set Up in Arkansas: Group Will Deal With Secondary Level Problems." Associated Press, December 15, 1957, in Arch Ford Collection, University of Arkansas Libraries Special Collections.

"Education Department Completes Its Move." *Arkansas Democrat*, August 29, 1969.

"Education Department Considered Too Small to Help 385 Districts." *Arkansas Gazette*, July 3, 1976.

"Education Department Goes on TV." *Arkansas Gazette*, November 29, 1959.

"Education Department Integrated." *Arkansas Gazette*, June 3, 1965.

"Education Department to Expand: Addition of Five Supervisors Would Raise Federal Aid." *Arkansas Democrat*, January 5, 1959.

"Education TV May Start Early." *Arkansas Gazette*, April 5, 1963.

"Educational TV Group to Meet." *Arkansas Democrat*, July 8, 1958.

"Educational TV Target Date Set as July, 1964." *Arkansas Gazette*, March 20, 1963.

"Educators Back School Report." *Arkansas Gazette*, August 25, 1978.

"Enforcement Not State Job, Ford Tells Howe." *Arkansas Gazette*, July 6, 1966.

"Excellent Appointment." *Arkansas Democrat*, January 17, 1953.

"Faubus Calls GACE to Its Second Job: Improve Teaching." *Arkansas Gazette*, May 10, 1957.

Faubus, Orval. Presentation at Conway High School, February 27, 1986.

"Faubus Praises Morrilton as Site of Vocational School." *Arkansas Gazette*, February 20, 1962.

"Faubus Sees School Chaos If Tax Killed." *Arkansas Gazette*, May 9, 1957.

Fersh, George and Mildred. *Bessie Moore: A Biography*. Little Rock: August House, 1986.

Ford, Arch. "Arkansas Education Proud of 'Recognition.'" *Arkansas Democrat*, January 27, 1963.

———. "Kindergarten Amendment." *Education Newsmagazine*, October 1968.

———. "Leaders in Education." *Education Newsmagazine*, February 1967.

———. "More Consolidation." *Arkansas Democrat*, June 25, 1953.

"Ford Again Elected to Economic Group." *Arkansas Gazette*, November 13, 1968.

"Ford Announces That He'll Retire as Education Director." *Log Cabin Democrat*, September 8, 1978.

"Ford Asked to Explain Inaction." *Arkansas Democrat*, November 22, 1953.

"Ford Declines Bid to Discuss New Bias Rules." *Arkansas Gazette*, April 12, 1966.

"Ford Defends Separate Board for School TV." *Arkansas Gazette*, June 25, 1963.

"Ford Emphasizes Role of Economics in State Schools." *Arkansas Gazette*, July 13, 1963.

Ford, Joe. Interview by Gabe Gentry for Economics Arkansas, April 2015.

"Ford Names 1st Consultant on School Desegregation; He's a Veteran Educator." *Arkansas Gazette*, April 16, 1968.

"Ford Opposes Racial Rider on School Bill: Tells House Group Whites Also Denied Equal Opportunities." *Arkansas Gazette*, June 19, 1963.

"Ford Pledges Help With Adjustment to Desegregation." *Arkansas Gazette*, May 2, 1972.

"Ford Praises Legislative Acts on Education." *Arkansas Gazette*, March 19, 1963.

"Ford Says Plan for Equalization Excels Cherry's." *Arkansas Gazette*, March 6, 1955.

"Ford Says Ratings Misleading Public on School Quality." *Arkansas Gazette*, December 21, 1966.

"Ford Says Schools Can't Look for Help from Legislature." *Arkansas Gazette*, February 4, 1976.

"Ford Says State Can Afford Free Textbooks as Well as Raise for Teachers." *Arkansas Gazette*, October 11, 1966.

"Ford Says State Must Plan for Kindergarten Program." *Arkansas Gazette*, December 5, 1962.

Ford, Scott. Interview by Gabe Gentry for Economics Arkansas, April 2015.

"Ford Seeks Re-election." *Arkansas Gazette*, March 12, 1972.

"Ford Sees Finances as Top Problem." *Arkansas Democrat*, June 6, 1954.

"Ford Slated to Be New School Head." *Arkansas Democrat*, January 9, 1953.

"Ford Spurns Raise Unless Teachers Also Get More." *Arkansas Gazette*, March 8, 1955.

"Ford Supports Move to Form Two Year Colleges." *Arkansas Gazette*, March 19, 1964.

"Ford to Run Drive for College's Funds." *Arkansas Gazette*, July 16, 1968.

"Ford to Urge Public School for Retarded." *Arkansas Gazette*, July 15, 1972.

"Ford Views School Integration Order." *Arkansas Democrat*, November 9, 1967.

"Former Commissioner of Education Dies at 81." *Arkansas Gazette*, June 6, 1987.

"Former Education Department Director, Mr. Ford, Dies at 81." *Log Cabin Democrat*, June 5, 1987.

Forster, Bobbie. "Amazing Progress in Education in Decade Cited by Commissioner." *Arkansas Democrat*, March 24, 1959.

"Free High School Textbooks Come into Limelight Again." *Arkansas Gazette*, March 11, 1962.

"Free Textbooks in High School Are Proposed." *Arkansas Gazette*, October 14, 1965.

"Free Textbooks Major Priority, Governor Declares." *Arkansas Gazette*, September 2, 1972.

"Free Textbooks Recommended if Funds Found." *Arkansas Gazette*, October 12, 1966.

"Freedoms Foundation Will Honor A. W. Ford for Work in Education." *Arkansas Gazette*, May 1, 1964.

"Funding Is Voted for Kindergartens, Junior Colleges." *Arkansas Gazette*, April 4, 1973.

"Future of Education Great, Dr. Ford Says." *Daily Banner-News*, January 8, 1975.

"GACE Session Maps Strategy for School Aid." *Arkansas Gazette*, December 1, 1956.

Garrison, Jerol. "16 Years after Ruling, Integration Nears Completion in State Schools." *Arkansas Gazette*, August 30, 1970.

Garrison, Jerol. "Cooperation Is Ordered in Planning." *Arkansas Gazette*, July 10, 1970.

Gillam, Dorothy. Interview by Gabe Gentry for Economics Arkansas, April 2015.

Gillam, Dorothy. Interview by Scott Lunsford for Pryor Center, August 3, 2011.

"Governor Says He Favors Kindergarten for Public." *Arkansas Gazette*, December 30, 1964.

"Governor Signs Textbook Bill." *Arkansas Gazette*, March 16, 1967.

"Guidelines on Discipline to Be Sought, Ford Says." *Arkansas Gazette*, January 17, 1975.

Harris, Sam. "State's Pattern to be Set by District Tribunals; Decision Lauded by Most." *Arkansas Gazette*, June 1, 1955.

Harwood, Bill, ed. "Arch Ford." In *School Days: Contemporary Views of Arkansas Education*. Little Rock: Winthrop Rockefeller Foundation, 1978.

"HEW Tells South 1969 Is Deadline for Desegregation." *Arkansas Gazette*, November 9, 1967.

"Honorary Doctorate for Two." *Baptist Magazine*, May 1, 1962.

"House Okays Bills on Educational TV." *Arkansas Gazette*, March 8, 1963.

"Inequities in Education Up for Study: Survey to Cover Equalization and Segregation Issues." *Arkansas Democrat*, December 14, 1953.

"It's the Durable Arch Ford and His Door Is Always Open." *Nashville News*, April 12, 1977.

"JBC Approves Appropriation for Textbooks." *Arkansas Gazette*, March 13, 1973.

Johnson, Kenneth. "Educators to Study Curricula: Agriculture, Home Economics to Be De-Emphasized." *Commercial Appeal*, January 4, 1958.

"Johnson to Become President of Security Savings and Loan." *Log Cabin Democrat*, December 13, 1977.

"Jones Denies Role in Vote Against Ford." *Arkansas Gazette*, December 11, 1960.

"KATV's Offer Accepted; State Reveals Program for Education Network." *Arkansas Gazette*, March 9, 1978.

Kaufman, Ken. "Arkansas Integration Must Wait, Ford Says." *Arkansas Democrat*, July 1, 1954.

"Kindergarten Bill Favored after Senators Change Vote." *Arkansas Gazette*, January 20, 1973.

"Kindergarten Bill Signed by Bumpers." *Arkansas Gazette*, February 9, 1973.

"Kindergarten Bill Stirs Disorder." *Arkansas Gazette*, April 2, 1971.

"Kindergarten Program Backed by Commissioner." *Log Cabin Democrat*, November 15, 1967.

"Kindergartens Run by Aid Are Approved." *Arkansas Gazette*, October 23, 1965.

"Leaders in Education." *Education* 83 (May 1963).

Ledbetter, Calvin R. "The Fight for School Consolidation in Arkansas, 1946-1948." *Arkansas Historical Quarterly* 65 (Spring 2006).

"Legislative Battle on Kindergarten Set Next Week." *Arkansas Democrat*, April 4, 1973.

"Legislators Balk at Idea of Public Kindergarten." *Arkansas Democrat*, January 7, 1973.

"'Left Wing' Textbook Probe Set." *Arkansas Democrat*, November 22, 1953.

"Letting Governor Take Over School Unwise, Ford Says." *Arkansas Gazette*, November 1, 1969.

"LR District May Get Experimental Program in Economic Education." *Arkansas Gazette*, January 5, 1966.

McDermott, Cecil. Letter, November 5, 1974, in Arch Ford Collection, scrapbook 50, University of Arkansas Libraries Special Collections.

McMath, Sid. Letter, March 6, 1975, in Arch Ford Collection, scrapbook 50, University of Arkansas Libraries Special Collections.

"Mobile Education." *Arkansas Gazette*, January 7, 1973.

"Mobile Machine Shop Training Unit." *Education Newsmagazine* (October 1970).

"Morrilton Plugs Itself as Site of Tech School." *Arkansas Gazette*, February 9, 1962.

"Most Teachers Have a Degree." *Arkansas Gazette*, March 10, 1970.

"Negro Leader Disputes Ford on Integration." *Arkansas Gazette*, January 29, 1966.

"New Desegregation Directive May Affect About a Fourth of State Schools, Ford Says." *Arkansas Gazette*, November 9, 1967.

"New State Vocational School Is Sought by Several Cities." *Arkansas Gazette*, November 9, 1963.

Old State House Museum Associates. "Exhibit: The Civilian Conservation Corps in Arkansas." *Faulkner Facts and Fiddlings* (1995): 41.

"'Oust Ford' Plan Wins ALC Okay." *Arkansas Gazette*, December 8, 1960.

Oxley, Howard W. "Education in Civilian Conservation Corps Camps." http://catalog.hathitrust.org/Record/003240357 (accessed March 13, 2016).

"Panel Approves Goals Statement for Education." *Arkansas Gazette*, November 10, 1977.

Patten, David A., and Jeffrey L. Rodengen. *The Legend of Alltel*. Fort LauderdaLE, FL: Write Stuff Syndicate, 2001

"Pay Raise for Educators in State Averages $987." *Arkansas Gazette*, February 12, 1976.

Pearson, Arch E. "Memories of the Wooster Community." *Faulkner Facts and Fiddlings* (1964).

Penny, Nancy. "The Thomas Francis Clements Family." In *Faulkner County: Its Land and People*. Conway, AR: Faulkner County Historical Society, 1986.

"Pine Bluff Man to Head School at Morrilton." *Arkansas Gazette*, March 13, 1962.

"Pine Bluff School Draws 509 Students." *Commercial Appeal*, February 28, 1960.

"Plan to Help Handicapped Approved." *Arkansas Gazette*, September 12, 1967.

"Plans for $750,000 Educational TV Network Are Unveiled." *Commercial Appeal*, July 6, 1964.

"Pryor Got Most Items He Wanted." *Jonesboro Sun*, August 7, 1977.

"Pulaski Vocational Technical School to Open at Its New Location January 19." *Arkansas Gazette*, January 11, 1976.

"Quality Education Act, With Jones' Change Passed 26-1 in Senate." *Arkansas Gazette*, March 2, 1969.

Reed, Roy. *Faubus: The Life and Times of an American Prodigal*. Fayetteville: University of Arkansas Press, 1997.

———. "House Rejects Ford Pay Raise: Van Dalsem Persists, Wins His Vendetta." *Arkansas Gazette*, March 7, 1961.

"Reorganization Plan Stirs Fuss in GACE: Ford Leads Opposition to Plan for Penalties for Balky Districts." *Arkansas Gazette*, June 21, 1956.

"Reorganization Reverses 97 Years of Traditions." *Arkansas Gazette*, February 7, 1971.

"Ruling Means That Teachers Get an Extra $600,000." *Arkansas Gazette*, August 5, 1953.

Ryan, Loyd D. "School Consolidation: A Giant Step for Learning." *Log Cabin Democrat Weekender*, March 9, 1979.

"School Bill Goes to Pryor." *Arkansas Gazette*, March 2, 1977.

"School Seekers Heard." *Arkansas Gazette*, August 2, 1957.

"School Trends Noted by Ford." *Commercial Appeal*, April 4, 1963.

"School Quality Bill Introduced." *Arkansas Gazette*, January 14, 1969.

"School Unit Study in Every County Okayed by Senate." *Arkansas Gazette*, February 14, 1963.

"Schools Face Financial Bind in Classes for Handicapped." *Arkansas Gazette*, March 7, 1976.

"Security Expects to Receive Bids in December." *Log Cabin Democrat*, November 24, 1967.

Security Savings and Loan Financial Statement, June 30, 1968, in Arch Ford Collection scrapbook 24, University of Arkansas Libraries Special Collections.

"Security Savings and Loan Names Three Officers." *Log Cabin Democrat*, April 11, 1975.

"Separate But Equal Policy Set for Schools." *Arkansas Democrat*, June 14, 1954.

"Seven Times More Negroes Attend Integrated Schools." *Arkansas Gazette*, January 1, 1966.

Shannon, Karr. "Run of the News: A School Man for the Top Education Job." *Arkansas Democrat*, January 7, 1953.

Shofner, Joan, director of Advancement Research, University of Central Arkansas, email August 28, 2015.

Shores, Elizabeth. "The Arkansas Children's Colony at Conway: A Springboard for Federal Policy on Special Education." *Arkansas Historical Quarterly* 57 (1998).

"Special Education and How It Works." *Arkansas Gazette*, January 2, 1977.

Smith, Sandra Taylor. "The Civilian Conservation Corps in Arkansas 1933-1942." Arkansas Historic Preservation Program.

Speaker, Ed. Letter, December 2, 1978, Arch Ford Collection, scrapbook 73, University of Arkansas Libraries Special Collections.

Speakman, Joseph M. "Into the Woods: The First Year of Civilian Conservation Corps." *Prologue* 38, no. 3 (Fall 2006).

"Special Education Needed by Many School Children." *Arkansas Democrat*, November 3, 1969.

"Standards Revised for Certification of State Teachers." *Arkansas Gazette*, March 10, 1970.

"State 5th in Proportionate Support of Schools." *Arkansas Gazette*, June 5, 1960.

"State a Leader in Teaching of Economics." *Arkansas Gazette*, January 19, 1966.

"State Board Approves 60-Hour Plan for School Administrators." *Arkansas Gazette*, September 9, 1963.

"State Board of Education Approves Plan to Improve Job Opportunities for Blacks, Women." *Arkansas Gazette*, March 3, 1974.

"State Board Moves to Raise Standards in Teacher Hiring." *Arkansas Gazette*, June 10, 1963.

"State Board Revises Setup in Education." *Arkansas Gazette*, August 29, 1966.

"State Committed to Desegregation, Ford Declares." *Arkansas Gazette*, April 2, 1968.

"State Complex to Honor Ford." *Arkansas Gazette*, May 20, 1969.

"State Losing Funds." *Arkansas Gazette*, December 13, 1977.

"State May Get Federal Funds for Education." *Arkansas Gazette*, September 9, 1958.

"State Prisons Get $200,000 for Education." *Arkansas Gazette*, March 24, 1970.

"State Relieved of Pressure." *Arkansas Gazette*, March 22, 1973.

"State Schedules Adult Schooling Trial Program." *Arkansas Gazette*, July 14, 1961.

"State Teachers Win Awards in Economics." *Arkansas Gazette*, October 26, 1967.

"State Vocational Training Increase Needed, Funds Lacking, Ford Says." *Arkansas Gazette*, September 12, 1961.

"State's Economic Education Promoted by Sears, Roebuck." *Arkansas Gazette*, June 19, 1963.

"Substantial Gains in Arkansas Education." *Arkansas Gazette*, September 23, 1973.

"A Survivor in the Spoils Jungle: Veteran Educator Enjoys Relaxing around Home." *Arkansas Gazette*, January 10, 1979.

"Table 5.3. Types of state and district requirements for kindergarten entrance and attendance, by state, 2014." https://nces.ed.gov/programs/statereform/tab5_3.asp (accessed March 14, 2016).

"Teachers in Arkansas Schools Are Acquiring More Education." *Arkansas Gazette*, December 11, 1960.

"Tech School a Big Help, Pryor Says." *Arkansas Gazette*, July 6, 1966.

"Technical School Has 224 Enrollees." *Arkansas Gazette*, October 14, 1959.

"Tuesday Meeting Will Form Economic Education Council." *Arkansas Gazette*, February 25, 1962.

"Trade School at Morrilton Dedicated." *Arkansas Gazette*, August 26, 1963.

"Trade School Bid Opening Set for May 17." *Arkansas Gazette*, March 15, 1966.

"Trade School Committee to be Named." *Arkansas Gazette*, September 11, 1963.

"Trade Schools Announced for Eight Areas." *Arkansas Gazette*, June 15, 1965.

"Training School to Be Available for All in State." *Arkansas Gazette*, July 7, 1963.

"Training Teachers for the Retarded." *Arkansas Democrat*, August 3, 1955.

Trower, Kathy. "Road Trips: Wooster Is an Integral Part of Faulkner County, Arkansas." *Arkansas Democrat-Gazette, River Valley and Ozark Edition*, July 18, 1999, 6R.

Tuchey, Matilda. "The Arkansas Angle: Arch Ford: His Learning Came the Hard Way." *Arkansas Gazette*, September 13, 1953.

Tuohey, Matilda. "Ax Swings High and Low in Education Department." *Arkansas Gazette*, June 14, 1955.

"Tyler to Head TV Commission." *Arkansas Gazette*, March 2, 1962.

Tyson, Van A. "Education Leader Is Veteran on Job: Ford Has Headed His Department for 21 Years." *Arkansas Democrat*, August 12, 1974.

"U.S. Tells South It Must Speed Up School Integration." *Arkansas Gazette*, March 8, 1966.

Valachovic, Ernest. "Educators Study State Operation of Kindergartens." *Arkansas Gazette*, June 18, 1961.

——. "Fuss Continues on Site Choice for New School." *Arkansas Gazette*, February 25, 1962.

——. "State Educators Seek to Improve Teachers' Caliber." *Arkansas Gazette*, April 14, 1959.

"Van Dalsem and the Education Proviso." *Arkansas Gazette*, December 18, 1960.

"Van Dalsem Off on a Trip; Ford Pulls a Comeback." *Arkansas Gazette*, February 12, 1960.

"Vast Improvement in Schools Coming Soon, Ford Says." *Arkansas Gazette*, August 22, 1965.

"Vo-Tech Here Gets New Name." *Pine Bluff Commercial*, March 18, 1966.

Ward, John L. "Arch W. Ford: A Quiet Survivor of the Political Maelstrom." *Log Cabin Democrat*, January 10, 1979.

Ward, John L. "Special Education Needs Charting of New Course." *Arkansas Democrat*, February 16, 1961.

"Who's Who in U.S. Business to Conduct State Seminar." *Arkansas Gazette*, June 9, 1963.

Williams, Fay. "Archie Ford, State Commissioner of Education." *Arkansans of the Year*, 1951–54. Little Rock: C. C. Allard and Associates, 1954.

Williams, Fay. "Introducing Archie Ford, State Commissioner of Education." *Arkansas Democrat Sunday Magazine*, July 19, 1953.

Williams, Justin, Sr. "The Clements of Wooster." *Faulkner Facts and Fiddlings* 21 (1979).

"Won't Interfere in Picking School Site, Faubus Says." *Arkansas Gazette*, August 22, 1957.

Wooten, Jim. Interview with Gabe Gentry for Economics Arkansas, April 2015.

"Yesterdays—25 Years Ago." *Log Cabin Democrat*, May 7, 2005.

Index

About the Author

Cindy Burnett Beckman is a recently retired high school social studies teacher. After receiving an MA in history from the University of Central Arkansas in 1985, she taught history and economics at Conway High School in Conway, Arkansas, for thirty years. In 2001, she was named the national Junior Achievement Economics Teacher of the Year. Together with her husband, Ron, she also taught economics in Tajikistan in June 2001 as part of a Winrock International initiative to provide economic education to former Soviet countries.

Beckman writes *A Look Back*, a weekly local history column for the *Log Cabin Democrat* newspaper, and is on the board of the Faulkner County Historical Society. She has self-published two books: *A Taste of Arkansas: Restaurants of Conway, Faulkner, Perry, Pope and Yell Counties: A Guide to Great Restaurants and the People Who Run Them* (1993) and *By the Forks of the Cadron: Living in a Place Called Pleasant Valley* (1999).